The Apple Core Enigma and Other Short Stories
By David Ryan
Book Cover design by Charlotte Hultin
© 2016 David Ryan

ISBN: 978-2-9700936-4-0

The Apple Core Enigma
and Other Short Stories

David Ryan

Contents

GRAVE MATTER

Jason Branaghan stared fixedly at the sheet of paper he was holding. He, of course, knew it by heart and had read it countless times over many years. Two phrases jumped out at him: 'at a convenient location' and 'Friday, 10th July, 2015.' Today was that date.

Branaghan worked for the BBC, hosting an hour-long TV programme three times a week. His image was that of a young, dynamic, witty man-about-town and, although his impeccable Savile Row appearance bore witness to this effect, he was at this particular moment ill-at-ease and apprehensive. He picked up a magazine from his coffee table and scanned it superficially. He began reading an article but was interrupted by the ringing of the doorbell.

He greeted his visitor warmly, "Jeremy! I'm delighted to see you. How are you?"

"Hello, Jason. I'm very well. It's good to see you, too. You've hardly changed, you know."

Within two minutes the doorbell rang again. Branaghan answered it and this time admitted a stout, rather shabbily dressed individual with unkempt hair and shapeless trousers whom they were nevertheless obviously very pleased to see. "Matthew. How are you? Come on in. Great to see you. Say, you've put on a few kilos, haven't you?"

"That," explained Matthew Fingleton, rubbing his expanding waistline affectionately, "is the result of six years of happy married life with three kids to show for it."

They were all in their late 20's but, to look at them, you would never have guessed that these three men could have so much in common and yet they shared a secret unbeknown to anyone else; theirs was a bond that could never be dissolved.

Branaghan brought a decanter of whisky over from a sideboard, set down three crystal glasses and poured generous helpings into each of them. Matthew Fingleton looked at his drink wistfully and muttered, "You know, this will be the first strong drink I've had since . . . ." He cut himself short before adding, "Well, you know what I mean."

"We know, Matthew, but more of that later. Meanwhile tell us about yourself. What subject do you teach?"

"History, with a bit of Economics."

Fingleton then outlined the drab existence of a Sussex schoolmaster, before, in turn, addressing Wilkins, "What about you, Jeremy? What do you do?"

Wilkins was an impetuous, outspoken, somewhat brash individual who had inherited a fortune and bought a chain of garages. He clearly welcomed the

2

opportunity to tell the others just how well he felt he had done.

They both knew all about Branaghan as he appeared so often on television: quiz programmes, current affairs, interviews, even sports commentaries. He seemed to be the ultimate all-rounder and his was a household name. They now admired his elegant apartment that boasted many designer features as was befitting for someone with such a profile.

They had been in occasional email contact for a number of years but this was their first meeting in a decade, since that fateful evening. They now exchanged such snippets of information as friends invariably do after a long separation.

All the while Fingleton struggled to get down the unaccustomed liquor without showing discomfort. Finally he said, "At least we've all managed to keep the agreement."

"Yes," snapped the rumbustious Wilkins, "but I'm not sure that talking about it will do us any good."

"That's something we'll have to see," said Branaghan. "It might at least be cathartic and I think we need to review what happened. After all, we've had to live with it for the past ten years."

But now that they were all together again and could speak freely, each one felt a certain reluctance about being the first to break the ice.

"Who would ever have guessed what was going to happen?" ventured Fingleton. "I presume neither of you has ever said anything. I certainly haven't."

"Of course not!" interjected Wilkins, showing annoyance at being asked such a question. "Why on earth would we? And I'm still not convinced we should talk about it now."

"I don't agree with you, Jeremy," said Branaghan. "I don't see how we can avoid discussing it tonight. After all, that's what we're here for, isn't it?"

Wilkins shrugged his shoulders in resignation and the ensuing silence was finally broken by Fingleton's philosophical ponderation, "Jason's right, Matthew. We can't pretend it didn't happen and nothing will ever change that. And let's face it; whichever way you look at it, we did kill Old Ben, albeit accidentally."

"It was a complete accident, the way it happened," snapped Wilkins. "We didn't mean to kill him, did we?"

"No, but we are nevertheless responsible," acceded Branaghan. "We caused his death and I think we have to face the facts."

The facts they had to face were still unbearable to them but they gradually began to recall in painful detail everything that had transpired that terrible evening ten years before.

They had been sixth form students at Granston Park College and had just taken their final exams before going on to university. They were due to go their separate ways the following day and had walked into the nearby village that evening to celebrate their forthcoming emancipation with a drink or two.

It was nearly 11pm when they made their way back to school and they decided to take the short cut along the river path, despite the muddy conditions underfoot following a day of rain. As the path entered the school grounds, it changed to a gravel surface and was separated from the river by an ornamental balustrade. Impressive though it was, the balustrade had, with the passing of time, started to crumble in places and was in need of repair.

A little further along the path they came upon Ben, the school gardener and odd-job man. Ben was in his early sixties, a simple individual who was approaching retirement. He was something of a Jekyll and Hyde character: friendly, sociable, almost affectionate most of the time, but confused, unpleasant and even aggressive when he had been drinking. Such was the case now. He lived on his own in a cottage in the school grounds and was making his way home.

"What are you lot doing down here?!" Ben blurted out as they caught up with him. "You know this is out of bounds for students. I'm going to have to report this, you know." He added something about 'spoiled brats', all the while wagging an accusatory finger in their direction.

In 24 hours' time they would have left school, so they just laughed at Ben's threat and decided to have a bit of fun at his expense. Now it was their turn to threaten him. They slowly advanced and started to close in on him, laughing as he nervously retreated. Branaghan was carrying his telescopic umbrella and used it to poke Ben in the chest a number of times. Ben stepped back unsteadily and when he reached the edge of the path he groped for support, unfortunately at exactly the point where the balustrade was broken. Instead of finding a handhold to steady himself, he stumbled over the wall and fell into the river.

The three friends initially found this very amusing but, by the time they stopped laughing and looked into the river, everything had gone quiet. There was no sign of Ben anywhere, nor was there any movement in the water. They peered over the balustrade but could see nothing; it was particularly dark that night as there was no moon. They called out his name but heard nothing in reply. They had no idea what to do. In fact there seemed to be very little they could do. After a few minutes panic set in. They looked at each other in horror and started to move back from the river. In their anxiety to leave the scene, Branaghan tripped, fell and dropped his umbrella.

They walked back up through the vast school park to the complex of buildings housing the accommodation block where they had left a ground-floor window unlatched for easy access. All the while they discussed their predicament, trying to convince each other that what had happened was purely an accident, that they weren't really responsible for it and that there was no need to mention it to anyone else.

They sat around in the sixth form common room for a long while, looking at the situation from every possible angle. Finally they agreed to continue as usual but not to be seen together in the immediate future. They mistakenly thought that what had happened would be covered by the Statute of Limitations so that after ten years they would not even face prosecution. They wrote a pact on the common room computer and printed off three copies. It read:

6

'We, the undersigned, promise to meet up at a convenient location in the evening of Friday, 10th July, 2015, to discuss a grave matter of mutual concern'.

They all signed the three copies and retained one each. Next morning they unenthusiastically attended their graduation ceremony before wishing each other well and going off to their various destinations.

That same day Ben's body was found on the top edge of the weir some fifty metres downriver from where he had fallen in. Later there had been a perfunctory police inquiry and a postmortem and it was assumed that Ben had fallen and hit his head while trying to cross the weir on his way home. The conclusion was accidental death by drowning.

That was ten years ago to the day. Now, having gone over the whole series of events again, Wilkins said, "Listen. Don't you think we could change the subject now? After ten years of guilt, fear, lying and sleepless nights, we've just re-lived the whole damn thing again and I for one have had enough."

"You're right, Jeremy," agreed Branaghan. "In fact I got my cleaner to prepare us something to eat earlier on. I'll go and fetch it."

And he headed off towards the kitchen. Just then they heard a key turning in the front door and a slightly-built individual walked into the lounge. Surprised at hearing the door open, Branaghan came back into the room to see who it was. For a moment he did a double take, then he froze and exclaimed in horror, "Parker! How the hell did you get in here?"

"Simple, really. Through the door. I've been outside listening to your conversation for the past hour or so and now I have some news for you. We're all going to sit down here quietly for a while and just wait. The police will be here a little later and I'm sure they will be interested to hear everything you have been saying."

"Don't be a fool, Parker. You don't think we're going to repeat all that, do you?" asked Fingleton.

"No need to," came the reply. "I've already solved that one."

"What do you mean?" interjected Wilkins.

"Well, let me explain it all to you. I became suspicious of you three when I got back to school that night 10 years ago and noticed three pairs of wet, muddy shoes covered in gravel. Your big mistake, though, was not closing down the computer in the Common Room so I just helped myself to a copy of your pledge. Although I always suspected it, I have been waiting for ten years to be able to prove what you did. You'll be surprised, Branaghan, to learn that I also work for the BBC. Oh, I don't do anything glamorous like you. I'm just a technician but, if I say so myself, quite a good one. I am also good with computers and easily hacked into yours. I read all the correspondence between the three of you so knew that you would be meeting up here tonight."

"Come to the point, will you?" said Branaghan.

"Oh, I will. Don't you worry. A few weeks ago, I followed you to the gym where you work out, Branaghan. While you were doing your thing, I went to the changing rooms, found your keys and took imprints of anything that looked remotely like a door key. Fortunately one of them was exactly that. That's why I was able to walk in here just now. A few days ago I sussed this place out and concealed a recording device over there behind that bookcase. I called in earlier on before you came home, Branaghan, and turned the machine on."

"What are you talking about?" asked Wilkins aggressively, "I'm going to check this out."

"No, you're not, Wilkins. You just sit down again and stay there. In fact all of you go and sit on that sofa and don't get up."

In saying this, Parker produced a small handgun from his inside pocket and sat down opposite them. He had always felt that the others despised him when they had been at school and he had seen this as an opportunity to get equal with them. He had even been prepared to take the risk of acquiring the firearm that he now brandished in their general direction. They did as they were ordered.

"You always made it clear you had no time for me so I thought I'd teach you a bit of a lesson and let you face the consequences of what you did. Now all we have to do is wait a little longer, hand the recording over to the police and leave it to them. By the way, they'll be here at 10 o'clock. I've already arranged that. So we'll just sit down here and wait patiently until they come."

What the three friends didn't know about that fateful night was that a solitary figure had come along the riverside path some way behind them. William Parker. He was known to be a loner who had no real friends and seemed to resent anyone else who had; hence his dislike of his three classmates. They were all popular, sporty, and academically gifted while he was none of these things.

9

Parker had been close enough to make out three silhouettes that he thought he recognised in some sort of scuffle a little way ahead. When he reached the same spot himself he was astonished to come face to face with Ben who was dripping with water from head to toe, staggering along the path towards him. He had just climbed out of the water, having previously drifted a little way downriver and got caught up in some bulrushes by the bank. Ben saw Parker approaching and, in his immense relief, went to give him a drunken embrace, muttering something about 'three little rich kids' pushing him in the river and not helping him to get out. The wet bear hug annoyed Parker who shoved him away violently. Ben advanced again, only to be repelled once more by an angry Parker. The gardener teetered backwards towards the balustrade and put his hand out to steady himself but once again there was nothing there and he fell into the river, striking his head on the broken stonework as he fell.

After a while, when Ben didn't reappear, Parker looked down into the river, only to discover him floating face-down and motionless on the surface of the water. This was Parker's chance to pin the blame for what he had just done on the three people he most detested. After all, the others must have assumed that they were responsible. Scapegoats! He could hardly believe his luck. He turned away and carried on along the path in the direction of the school buildings.

All these images now swirled around in his head as he sat down again facing the others who, in turn, were at a loss as to what to do next. Fingleton decided the best thing was to engage Parker in conversation to try to distract him and maybe even attempt to snatch the gun. After an appeal to his better nature that they knew would be fruitless and an exchange of pointless observations, Branaghan said, "We certainly didn't wish him any harm, you know. He might have been a sad character but he was really quite harmless. He seemed to be pleasant enough with everyone. Even to you, Parker, I imagine. What did you think of him, anyway?"

Parker stood up. "A pathetic individual. I can just picture him now going over that parapet, a bottle of alcohol in one hand and an umbrella in the other."

He turned and took a step in the direction of the bookcase as if to retrieve his recording but was stopped in his tracks by what he heard next.

Branaghan had sensed an unexpected opportunity, stood up and called out to Parker, "Wait a minute, Parker. How do you know all that? And what did you say just then about an umbrella? What umbrella?"

Parker spun round on his heel and confronted him angrily. He strode over to him and, in his fury, raised the gun and prodded him in the chest. "I didn't say anything about an umbrella. What are you talking about? It had been raining so I suppose he had an umbrella with him. What difference does that make anyway?"

"No difference, but he wasn't exactly the sort of person you'd expect to carry an umbrella, was he? What kind of umbrella was it?"

Parker's hand trembled visibly and his lips were flecked with saliva. "I don't know. One of those little folding things, I think."

"How would you know that?"

"I must have seen it, I suppose."

"Do you know something, Parker? That would have been my umbrella. I had dropped it earlier on that evening down by the river. If you saw it, as you say, and Ben was holding it, that means you must have seen him, alive, after us."

"You don't know what you're talking about," he fumed. "You're making all this up. You can't prove a thing, anyway."

"We don't need to. You've just proved it yourself. You were clearly the last person to see him alive, Parker. You can't deny that anymore."

"So you prove it!" he blurted again. "I can still get you three done you know. And, by the way, in case you don't know, the Statute of Limitations doesn't apply in this case. Anyway the police will be here soon and you can't do anything about that. OK. Perhaps I did see him down by the river and it might have been your umbrella. But so what? That doesn't change a thing. He was reeling all over the place and would probably have fallen in anyway."

"Yes, and maybe not."

"Well, there's no case against me. It was an accident. He just fell in the river again."

Fingleton was aghast at what he had just heard. "And you didn't even try to fish him out. Not only that but you could have admitted what had really happened and explained that it had just been an accident."

"True. But who do you think would have listened to me? In any case I thought it would be good to let you three take the blame."

"So we've had ten years of this for nothing," fumed Wilkins, "and you could have prevented it all the time."

"Tough!" came the reply. "Do you think I care? I thought I'd let you live with your 'grave matter' instead."

Parker was consumed by a mixture of anger and satisfaction. To show the others he still had the upper hand, he pointed the gun at each of them in turn with a threatening gesture, making sure they stayed in place and ordering them to sit down again. He glanced at his watch: three minutes to ten. A sense of power, of accomplishment, of excitement grew within him as he anticipated his big moment.

10 o'clock came and there was a ring on the doorbell. Parker beckoned to Branaghan to answer it and slipped the gun back in his pocket. A smartly dressed man walked into the room and introduced himself as Inspector Collins.

"And this is Sergeant Clayton," he added. "I understand you have some important information for me concerning the death of Ben Jenkins some years ago."

Fingleton's face was a picture of delight as he leaned over to Parker and whispered, "Do you want to know something, Parker? You forgot to turn off that recording just now. Let's see you get out of this one."

Parker's smirk of contentment turned to a look of absolute horror as he realised the life-changing mistake he had made. His face blanched as the Inspector looked steadily from one face to the other before asking, "Which one of you is William Parker?"

Parker did his best to look invisible but understood the situation in which he now found himself.

"I'm Jason Branaghan, Inspector. This is my apartment. That's William Parker. He forced his way in here earlier this evening." Then he added very deliberately, "I suggest you ask him to turn out his pockets and then look behind that bookcase over there. You'll find something that is sure to be of interest to you."

Inspector Collins followed these recommendations, asked Parker a few simple questions and could see that he clearly had enough evidence to take the next step:

"William Parker. I'm arresting you for illegally entering these premises and threatening those inside with a handgun. Other charges are likely to follow. Take him away, Sergeant."

WHAT'S IN A NAME?

Amina and her husband, Kintu, lived in a dusty village in the heart of Africa. They had been married for many years and, though they were very happy together, there was just one thing missing in their lives: a child of their own.

Everyone could see how good Amina was with other people's children and how much the children loved her. Nobody was more maternal. She desperately wanted a child of her own and had tried everything she could think of to make it happen: prayers, witch-doctors, special diet, herbal drinks – but all to no avail.

Then one day, when they had practically given up all hope, their lives changed dramatically. Amina quietly announced to her family and friends that she was pregnant. It seemed to be a miracle. The news quickly spread around the grass and earthen houses and the whole village gathered to celebrate with them and share their joy. Even the Chief came along wearing his best ceremonial robes.

The village had always been very poor but that was more than compensated for by the bonds of love and friendship that prevailed. To anticipate the forthcoming event together, the Chief convened all the villagers, and the square was packed with all 250 souls who lived there; the youngest was known to be less than a week old, the oldest thought to be well over 100 years. They chatted together well into the night and were already looking forward to welcoming the future arrival. It seemed to be the only topic of conversation. Months passed and the excitement increased as Amina's time approached.

On the expected day, the village midwife said she thought there would be good news by the end of the day. Everyone crept quietly around the village as they didn't want to disturb Amina's peace and concentration. They nonetheless greeted each other with a discreet word and a clear sense of expectancy. Then, just as the sun was setting and casting a soothing glow over the whole country, an infant's welcome cry penetrated the stillness of the balmy evening. The effort of observing a whole day's silence could be sustained no longer; the ecstatic villagers spontaneously started to sing, cheer, dance, and generally celebrate the new arrival.

Two days later Amina was strong enough to be up and about and it was with great pride that she and Kintu came out of their hut to present their baby boy to the rest of the village. Everyone said what a magnificent child he was, a perfect specimen.

During the next couple of days all her friends and neighbours just happened to be passing Amina's hut and called in to pay their respects and to admire the little one. They would have dearly loved to offer the family a gift but the village was extremely poor and there was practically nothing to give them.

Every single visitor asked the same question, "What are you going to call him?" And that's where the problem started. The new parents just couldn't make up their minds. Kintu was a very reserved individual; he never said much and was more than happy to leave the choice of name to his wife. She, in turn, used to think of a new name every few minutes but could not settle on any one in particular. It really had become something of a problem.

The Chief was starting to feel bad about not being able to offer a gift but, after considerable reflection, he had an inspirational idea. Although nobody could give much individually, he thought that, if everyone contributed something, no matter how little, they should be able to collect enough to mark the occasion in some way. Without exception every family gave what they could - a handful of grain, a few wooden beads, the odd coin or two, some fruit, beans, fufu, vegetables, a little woven basket - all of which could be sold at market.

Visiting the market meant a whole day's walk to get there and another to get back. They collected all their offerings together in a linen cloth and entrusted them to a young man who was known to be a strong athlete. He set off next day at dawn and strode out determinedly in the direction of the big town where there were said to be stone houses, lights in the streets and even a few cars. By evening he had managed to exchange all the items he had brought for a small amount of money which, for safety's sake, he slept on all night.

Next morning he was up very early and went down to the market place, going from stall to stall and examining all the wares he found on show there. He walked round it several times before deciding on what he thought would be an ideal gift for Amina. He thought the merchant was asking too much for it and in any case didn't have that amount of money to pay him. They sat down together and spent the next hour discussing a fair price. Finally they reached an agreement and shared a friendly drink of hibiscus juice to seal the deal. The messenger explained that he had a long way to go to get back home with his purchase so the stallholder carefully packed it in a cardboard box that he had, wrapped it in paper and wished him a safe return journey.

He felt sure that Amina would love what he had got for her and was so excited at the thought of getting back to the village that he actually ran most of the way. As a result he arrived in the early evening and went straight to the Chief's hut to show him his acquisition. The Chief was delighted, once again put on his best robes and summoned everyone to a meeting in the village square.

They didn't need to be asked twice. Within ten minutes they had all congregated to witness the presentation. The whole place was abuzz by the time Amina, who had been told to wait in her hut, arrived, carrying, of course, her nameless child in a wrap-round shawl. She had no idea what was happening, especially when everyone else formed a circle around her. The circle then opened up and into the centre stepped the Chief, carrying the beautifully wrapped package. Amina was bewildered but the Chief proudly delivered a carefully-rehearsed speech, explaining to her the reason for the unexpected assembly. After that he placed the package delicately between her hands and took a step back.

To a chorus of whispers, Amina nervously peeled off the paper, slowly opened the top of the box and withdrew the contents. There were gasps of astonishment, squeals of delight, murmurings of admiration as the wide-eyed villagers looked incredulously at each other and then back at Amina who was completely overcome. She stood there in their midst, proudly holding her new possession in her trembling hands, gazing down at a beautiful shiny brown and yellow object.

She drew in a deep breath and knew in an instant what she was going to call her infant son.

So, if one day you are travelling around Africa and you come upon someone called 'Teapot', you won't need to ask him why he has such strange name.

MAX

We reached the hotel a little after 5 o'clock on a warm Friday afternoon in June. Our own children had already fled the nest and, as we wanted to enjoy a quiet week by the sea, we had decided to take it well in advance of the school summer holidays. We had never visited this delightful seaside resort before and had chosen a small hotel that was just near the seafront, apparently well known for its friendly family atmosphere. It also claimed to provide every desirable service and convenience and certainly had excellent reviews on the Internet. As we walked up to the reception desk there was indeed an air of peace and calm, so much so that the whole place seemed to be deserted and there wasn't a sign of life.

Within seconds of pressing the call-bell, however, we were greeted by a cheery "Hello, can I help you?" The voice belonged to a dapper little fellow who was wearing a striking royal blue jacket and who positively bounced behind the desk, looking out at us through large popping eyes. His black hair was impeccably groomed and his delicate, pencil-like moustache twitched as his face lit up in his best receptionist smile.

"Oh, hello," said my wife. "We have a reservation for a week in the name of Johnson.

"You have, indeed," came the reply, "and may I say what a great pleasure it is to welcome you to our humble establishment, Mr and Mrs Johnson?"

"Thank you very much, Mr............."

"Oh no! Please call me Max. Everyone else here does."

"Thank you, Max," I enjoined.

I would guess the Cliff Haven Hotel had about 30 rooms and, as Max informed us that our 'outstandingly comfortable' room was located on the top floor, we accepted his offer to have our cases carried up for us. "An excellent idea," he said. "I'll just call the porter for you."

He then disappeared through a door at the back of the reception desk. We didn't have to wait long before there was a discreet clearing of the throat just behind us. We turned round to discover the porter, a small man wearing an elegant red jacket who was stooping down to pick up the cases. With the timing of an olympic weight-lifter he straightened up under his load and we could see that he bore a striking resemblance to Max, perhaps even his twin brother? His demeanour was similar, he had the same voice, same hair, same smile; he even had the same glint in his eye. We looked quizzically at each other, my wife with upraised eyebrows and furrowed brow, myself conscious of the fact that I was scratching the back of my head in disbelief.

When we reached the fourth floor, he opened the bedroom door with a flourish and delicately placed the cases at the end of the bed before giving us an ingratiating smile and proffering a bow worthy of a Shakespearean actor. He backed away towards the door and quietly exited the room.

We had said whilst registering that we would like to have dinner round about 7 o'clock and Max told us that we would be more than welcome to visit the bar for an aperitif before that, say from 6h30 onwards. We walked in exactly on cue and observed the barman who was sporting a bright green jacket busily arranging the bottles at the back of the bar. He noticed us in the mirror, spun round on his heel and stopped, facing us, with something akin to military precision. He smiled at us in a way that was quickly becoming familiar. My wife's jaw dropped and we probably both had the same thought: there can't possibly be three of them, not triplets!

"Good evening, Mr and Mrs Johnson. How delightful to see you again. What can I get for you?"

Though still bewildered, I ventured a tentative, "Max?"

"Glad to see that you remembered, Sir," he replied in a tone that would have done a primary school teacher proud when addressing a child who had just repeated that two times two make four. While we finished our drinks Max offered to take our dinner order for us. He particularly recommended the scallops to start with, followed by Beef Wellington.

We are very partial to both so readily followed his advice.

We had just sat down at our table when the swing doors from the kitchen opened and, dressed in an immaculate crisp white jacket, in walked the waiter. This time, of course, there was no real surprise and Max served our meal with exemplary efficiency.

It was a truly delicious dinner. We enjoyed it so much that we thought about calling for the cook to congratulate him on his excellent work but realised what the outcome would probably be. Instead I asked Max to convey our thanks to him personally and he walked off towards the kitchen wearing a very contented look on his face.

Throughout the week Max popped up everywhere you would expect him to and in some places you would never even have imagined. The hotel was practically empty of guests; come to think of it, I don't believe we ever saw anyone else. And in Max it was as though we had our own personal flunky. Time slipped by and all too soon the following Friday arrived, the day we were going home.

We were taking the afternoon train back and, as we still had the morning free, we decided to take advantage of one last hotel amenity. Their brochure boasted a chauffeur-driven car service so we decided to explore some of the surrounding countryside. Max did the formalities with us after breakfast and said we should be at the main entrance at 9 o'clock. Right on the stroke of nine a black limousine drew up at the door and we strolled over to it in eager anticipation.

Even though the driver was wearing a chauffeur's peak hat, I really didn't need to look twice to see who was sitting behind the wheel, dressed in an official-looking black jacket. A familiar voice politely asked us where we would like to go.

After an enjoyable excursion and a quick lunch, Max drove us to the station to catch our train home. As we slumped down in our carriage, my mind went over the events of the past week. On reflection I had two basic thoughts. Firstly, how lucky we had been with the weather and how enjoyable the week had been and, secondly, how grateful I felt towards a higher power that we had remained safe and in good health throughout our stay.

I shudder to think who would have appeared had we needed to ask for a priest, a doctor or the undertaker!

IN THE EYES OF A CHILD

Jeremy Harrington was a worried man. A multi-millionaire with every material comfort you can possibly think of and many more that don't even come to mind, he had never felt more depressed in his life.

Harrington was 49 years old, suave, charismatic, impressive in everything he did. In business he was ruthless, bold, innovative, uncompromising. He exuded confidence and was the classic example of the self-made man. After graduating in Economics from Cambridge, he had worked hard to build up a small amount of capital. He invested this shrewdly and watched it grow rapidly into a fortune. It multiplied at a phenomenal rate and he now counted it in billions. Among other things, his portfolio embraced shipping, banking, trading and real estate. Yet all this and the prestige that went with it could not rid him of the news he had just been told.

It had all started a few months before when Harrington felt a dull pain in his back. He had dismissed it as muscular discomfort, assuming that it would soon wear off but it didn't. Moreover he started suffering from extreme fatigue and even stopped playing golf which had hitherto been something of a passion. Unusually for him, he went to see his GP who did various tests and took a blood sample. Within the week he had been referred to a specialist.

He had just come from a consultation with Professor Cavendish, a distinguished oncologist. They had often played golf together and he knew that Cavendish would be completely frank with him as to the results. Now, as he faced him across the highly polished mahogany desk, the specialist came straight to the point. "I'm sorry, Jeremy, but the results are not good. I already suspected it but the scan has confirmed my worst thoughts. You have pancreatic cancer and unfortunately it is at an advanced stage and is inoperable."

Harrington was stunned: "How long do I have, Michael?"

"Difficult to say with any accuracy but probably two or three months, maybe six." Harrington was shocked to hear this and wondered if he would even see his next birthday.

He took his leave of the Professor, exited the Harley Street clinic and walked back to where he had told his chauffeur to wait. He slumped down into the back seat and said laconically, "Home please, John." The engine purred into life and John eased the Rolls away from the kerb and into the London rush hour traffic. Progress was slow and Harrington stared into the middle distance, all the while recalling some of the main events of his life: obtaining a double first from Cambridge, making his first million, his wedding, the birth of his children, Peter 25 and Rachel 22, their general falling out, his acrimonious divorce. The family situation was, he had to admit, largely of his own making; he had been obsessed with his work and rarely found time to spend at home with them. And then there was this afternoon.

He became conscious of the fact that the car had not moved for several minutes. John informed him that the GPS indicated that there was a total logjam in front of them and that it showed no sign of clearing any time soon. He sat there, lost in thought, looking fixedly through the tinted windows with glazed eyes. After a while his gaze fell on an illuminated hoarding featuring a group of ragged children with one child's emaciated face very prominent. It was particularly the large melancholic eyes that drew his attention. They seemed to be looking straight into his own, penetrating his mind, his heart, his very soul. Their eyes locked for several moments until Harrington noticed the caption beneath the child's head. It read: "Please help these desperate children: 5 pounds a month will stave off starvation." And those eyes pleading with him, beseeching him with a sort of hypnotic attraction! How could he refuse? He wanted to reach out to him, to do something to help but he had always been impervious to this sort of appeal.

John had been reading the evening newspaper as he sat in the car outside the clinic waiting for Harrington to return and, seeing that his employer now looked somewhat preoccupied, he asked him if he would like to read it. Harrington took it mechanically and started to leaf through the pages.

He was surprised to discover a half-page spread identical to the hoarding beside the car: the same group of children, the same message and, of course, the same haunting eyes, staring directly into his own.

Where was this child from? How old was he? Was he really starving? Perhaps he was just a young actor from a photographic agency. Would that really make any difference? Harrington looked back at the eyes again, intense, pleading, beguiling, and was filled with an overwhelming sense of collusion. Something had passed between them. His decision had been taken. He remembered a statistic he had seen recently in the media. It claimed that somewhere in the world a child dies unnecessarily every 5 seconds; that meant nearly one thousand children since he had left Dr Cavendish's surgery.

For years now he had watched his fortune grow and grow until it didn't really mean much anymore, just a series of statistics. He looked into the child's eyes again and smiled understandingly at him. His very existence was in the process of changing. He was filled with an intense sense of purpose. He took a deep breath and his mind was made up.

Slowly the Rolls started to move forward. As it did so Harrington turned and looked out of the back window. Those haunting eyes were still following his and he allowed himself a satisfied smile. The child, too, seemed to be smiling back at him as if to say "thank you."

Harrington glanced at his Patek Philippe. Almost 7 o'clock. It was still early enough to call another golfing friend, James Sullivan. Sullivan was a top lawyer. He had been a partner in Donaldson, Thorpe and Madison, the prestigious international law firm but had decided to leave them to set up his own exclusive practice. Sullivan saw who was calling him and, although it was getting late on a Friday evening, promptly picked up his phone. Harrington asked if they could meet the following morning to discuss a most urgent matter. Sullivan acquiesced and they agreed to meet in his chambers at 9 o'clock.

An hour and a half after their brief conversation, the big limousine, having left the London traffic behind, reached Harrington's mansion in Surrey. This was a secluded Georgian manor, set in a large wooded park and accessed through remote controlled wrought iron gates. In the absence of a family, he employed a personal assistant, Martin, who also acted as his butler and who, at his request, had prepared a plate of sandwiches for him. He retired to his room at 11 pm but spent most of the night awake, trying to work out some of the details of his project.

As he dressed next morning, Harrington was more convinced than ever that he had come to the right decision. 'Jeremy Harrington, Philanthropist'. Yes, he liked the sound of that! Sullivan was waiting for him when he arrived at the chambers and ushered him into his private study. Harrington carefully explained the situation to him and asked if he would agree to act on his behalf. Apart from nominal gifts to his ex-wife, his son and his daughter, the vast bulk of his wealth was to be attributed to a special fund. He said his decision was irrevocable.

They spoke about the different tragedies across the world affecting children that he would be able to address: famine, drought, homelessness, child labour, war zones, land mines, orphans, cancer, disease – the list was endless. Above all he said he would like to build, equip and staff children's hospitals in the third world. Sullivan was impressed by his friend's proposition and agreed to oversee the creation, development and running of the nascent Harrington Trust.

They met several times in the following weeks, usually at Harrington's house as he became weaker and less able to travel. After a while Sullivan was able to confirm that everything had been dealt with and was successfully in train. He went to see Harrington one more time and Martin was very happy to serve as witness to the signing of the new will.

Three days after their last meeting, as he was eating a light breakfast, Sullivan turned on the radio to listen to the news. He heard, "Here is the 8 o'clock news. The death has been announced of Jeremy Harrington, the renowned business tycoon, entrepreneur and property magnate. He died peacefully in his sleep last night and is rumoured to have bequeathed his entire fortune to the welfare of the world's underprivileged children. He was 50 yesterday."

TABLE FOR TWO

We had been walking for a couple of hours since eating our picnic lunch at the top of our climb and were thoroughly enjoying the descent. As we came out of a clump of trees, the path veered to the right and we found ourselves in a small clearing. The terrain here was flat and we were greeted by the welcome sight of a sturdy stone building that must once have been a farmhouse, a smallish south facing terrace, and a couple of tables each with four chairs and a sun umbrella proudly announcing a famous brand of lager. Exactly what we were looking for! It was about 4 o'clock and we were more than ready to take a break, absorb the warm afternoon sunshine and savour a refreshing beverage.

Jonathan and I had got up at 5 o'clock that morning to put in a hard day's hiking in the Lake District. We had reached the summit we were aiming for by midday, eaten a packed lunch of fruit and sandwiches and set out on the descent.

We sat down at one of the tables and were approached by a pleasant-looking woman wearing an apron and an enquiring smile.

"Good afternoon, gentlemen. What can I do for you?"

"Good afternoon," I replied. "We would like something to drink please."

"Oh yes, what would you like?"

"I will gladly settle for one of those," I answered, pointing up to the umbrella above our heads. "What about you, Jonathan?"

"Well, actually, I rather fancy a cup of tea please. Milk, but no sugar."

"Very well. I'll get them for you," and away she went.

We sat there admiring the view for a few minutes until she returned with our drinks on a small round tray and set them down on the table. After a while, seeing through the open door that she was busying herself in the kitchen, I called out to her, "Excuse me, but do you think we could have a few nibbles please: crisps, nuts, cheese straws, something like that?"

A stainless steel dish was duly delivered with a selection of savouries and a few olives. I ordered another beer and Jonathan poured himself a second cup of tea from the pot on the table.

Looking once more over the edge of the terrace down to the valley below, we realised that we no longer had too far to walk, felt very comfortable where we were and thought we would have a light meal before continuing on down to where we had left the car.

Again I called in the direction of the kitchen. "Do you think you could rustle up a little something to eat please, say, an omelette? Would that be OK for you, Jonathan?"

"Yes, fine."

"Could we have two omelettes then please? Just plain ones."

"I'll see what I can do, gentlemen." She disappeared into the kitchen again and we could hear the clatter of a pan and the sound of cooking eggs.

As she placed the cutlery before us, Jonathan said, "Would you mind filling our water bottles, please? They are running out and we still have a little way to go."

She went off with the bottles, filled them and brought them back with the omelettes, complete with a little sprig of parsley on top and a couple of sliced tomatoes.

Having enjoyed our meal, we thought it wise to set off in the direction of the valley before it started to get dark. I called for our waitress. "We have to be heading back now," I said. "Could you bring us the bill, please?"

"The bill? What bill?"

"The bill for everything we've drunk and eaten."

"Oh, I think there's been a misunderstanding," she said with a smile. "There's no bill. This is a private house!"

GUY FAWKES THE SECOND

Inspector Ashcroft was restless. He drummed his fingers impatiently on the top of his desk. Then, putting down the letter he had been reading, he leaned back in his chair and gazed into the middle distance. "You say no one was hurt, Hurley. At least that's something."

"That's right, Sir," replied Sergeant Hurley, the perfect foil for Ashcroft. In his early thirties, Hurley was sensitive, athletic and cool-headed. They had worked together for three years and made an excellent team. "Nobody was injured but apparently it made quite a mess of the shop. It went off at exactly 3 am, just as he said it would."

The explosion had occurred in a souvenir shop off the Strand. Initial investigation made it clear that it had been caused by a small, home-made bomb and triggered by the mechanism of a cheap alarm-clock. It had nevertheless been most effective.

The Inspector sighed and picked up the letter again. It was addressed to him personally and had been delivered the previous morning, April 1st. He had read it then but had quickly dismissed it as coming from some sort of crank who had nothing better to do. Perhaps some notion of an April Fool joke. He scanned the envelope again, 'Inspector Ashcroft, Scotland Yard, London', and read the letter once more:

DEAR INSPECTOR,
THIS IS JUST TO WARN YOU THAT ON SATURDAY APRIL 2ND AT 3 AM THERE WILL BE A LOUD BANG IN A LITTLE SHOP. CONSIDER THIS AS A GIFT FROM ME. YOU WILL HEAR FROM ME THREE MORE TIMES. THINGS WILL GET BIGGER AND BETTER. GUY FAWKES.

It was written on cheap paper and had been typed entirely in capital letters. The information in it was correct: April 2nd, 3 in the morning, explosion, small shop. Clearly he was not dealing with a joker after all. Before, he had found the words 'consider this as a gift from me' to be meaningless but now he understood; the shop in question was called 'The Gift Shop' and it was very clear that the writer's words could no longer be taken lightly.

As he had feared, there were no fingerprints, nor any DNA on the letter apart from his own, and neither the letter nor the envelope provided any information that helped the inquiry to progress in any way. Nor was it possible to trace the origin of the paper. Ashcroft was no further on.

It was nearly two years since Ashcroft had taken a holiday and his brow was more furrowed than usual. He had arranged to have a fortnight off later in the month to go walking and fishing in the Cotswolds but it now seemed that might have to wait. He had never married, nor ever seriously considered it; his whole existence had been devoted to his work. Forty-seven years of age, sixteen as Inspector, he was highly regarded by his colleagues, despite his idiosyncrasies and taciturn approach. They admired his tenacity and acknowledged that it had solved many a puzzling case when all seemed lost, and they were content to let him work in his own particular way.

His bushy eyebrows narrowed to a frown as he absent-mindedly twirled his pen in concentration. He decided that the other cases he was working on would have to wait; Guy Fawkes certainly wouldn't, and he had to get a lead on him. Why had his correspondent chosen that name? Why had he addressed the letter to him personally? He called Sergeant Hurley and told him they were going to pay a visit to "The Gift Shop."

The report had been accurate: the shop was indeed a shambles. The bomb had exploded in a corner where a large display cabinet containing glass ornaments had once stood. Anyone could easily have placed a small package behind it or in one of the nearby drawers without being noticed. The owner of the shop, David Goldberg, was visibly shaken. He was a small, balding man in his early 60's and he continually wrung his hands as he answered the

Inspector's questions. No, he hadn't noticed any strange customers the day before. No, nothing had seemed unusual to him. Did he have any known enemies? Certainly not! He was a respectable businessman. No, he didn't think he could give the police any useful information. Yes, he would, of course, contact them immediately if he remembered anything. Analysis of the fragments had produced no significant results and the shop was not equipped with CCTV.

As they drove back to Scotland Yard, Inspector Ashcroft muttered gruffly, "I don't suppose we can do much now except sit back and wait for the next one."

They didn't have to wait long.

The second letter was written in similar fashion and, of course, there were no fingerprints on it and no DNA. Like the first one, it had been posted in Central London. It read:

DEAR INSPECTOR,
I HOPE YOU APPRECIATED MY LITTLE GIFT. YOU WILL RECEIVE THIS ON APRIL 6TH. YOU WILL NOTICE THAT I AM BEING GENEROUS THIS TIME AS I AM GIVING YOU TWO DAYS. THE ACTION IS FOR THE 8TH. SOME TIME IN THE EVENING. IT'S THE ONLY WAY ACROSS TO THE OTHER SIDE OF THE STREET. GUY FAWKES

"The Other Side of the Street," repeated Sergeant Hurley wistfully. "That's the title of a new release and it's being premiered at the Leicester Square Odeon on Friday."

"Oh God, not a cinema!"

"Do you think he'll try something there, Sir?"

"I don't know. It seems too obvious when you think how vague he was last time. But we can't afford to leave anything to chance and we do have two days to get organised."

During the morning of the 8th, the cinema was thoroughly combed and Ashcroft was satisfied that nothing had as yet been hidden there. Police officers patrolling the area worked discreetly and no one who was asked to open a handbag, briefcase or any sort of package showed any objection. From midday onwards the area was heavily patrolled by officers who had received special instructions to be particularly vigilant.

Ashcroft himself sat with Sergeant Hurley in an unmarked patrol car near the Odeon. Just after 18h45 a communication came through informing him that there had been another explosion, this time a few minutes' drive from where he was waiting. He felt certain that Guy Fawkes must have carried out his second threat. This one appeared to be more serious than the first but it was only when they reached the scene that they realised the full extent of the horror.

Waiting for them was Officer Stevens, his face blanched, his trembling hands barely controllable. He had been called with PC Wright to examine a blue sedan that had been parked illegally on the yellow lines near a pedestrian crossing in Tudor Street. He spoke slowly and with evident emotion: "Wright walked up to the car, Sir, and as soon as he tried to open the door there was a deafening explosion. I ran up to try to help him but he was already dead. Killed outright."

"Thank you, Stevens. That'll be all for now," said Ashcroft and, as the officer walked dazedly back to his patrol car, the Inspector growled, but mainly to himself, "You bastard. I'll get you if it's the last thing I do," then more audibly to his Sergeant, "How the hell could we know what he was getting at? A pedestrian crossing! And now he's killed a policeman. I'll catch him, Hurley. I swear to God I will!"

Among the pieces of metal collected at the scene was the car's number plate and, later that evening, it lay buckled on Ashcroft's blotting pad in a transparent forensics bag. The intercom on his desk buzzed and this helped to calm his rising anger. He threw the switch.

"Mr Jessop is here, Sir."

"Then show him in," snapped the Inspector.

Mr Jessop's car had been stolen the night before and he had reported it to his local police station that same morning. He was surprised at being picked up in a police car and brought to Scotland Yard late in the evening for such a trifling matter. He was even more surprised when he noticed his twisted number plate on Ashcroft's desk.

"You say your car was stolen from outside your house during the night, Mr Jessop. Is that correct?"

"That's right Inspector, a blue Ford, 732 LTB, and I see you've found it already. I must say that Scotland Yard has been most . . . ."

The Inspector was in no mood for receiving compliments and cut Mr Jessop short to fire a few brief questions at him. His answers confirmed what was already quite clear. He had no connection with Guy Fawkes, his car had been randomly selected and he could not help the police in any way.

As the door closed on Mr Jessop, Ashcroft stared at his computer screen. The Guy Fawkes case was really taking shape now and it was the highly-organised planning and cold-blooded execution of it that so disturbed and mystified the Inspector. He seethed at the thought of his double failure; despite being warned on both occasions he had been incapable of taking the least preventative action. This had now resulted in the death of one of his colleagues and the threat seemed to be ever increasing. So far, all his enquiries had led to nothing and he was no nearer to arresting the perpetrator than he had been that Friday morning when he had nonchalantly tossed aside the first letter.

Special arrangements had been made with the Royal Mail to give absolute priority to all letters addressed to Inspector Ashcroft; this meant that he gained a few extra hours to assess the situation and work on a strategy. As he had heard nothing from his correspondent for over a week he began to hope that perhaps he had been frightened off by the death of PC Wright. This hope was brutally dashed, however, on April 19th when Sergeant Hurley handed him a familiar-looking envelope that had just been delivered. With a feeling of inevitability he slit it open and withdrew the contents. It read:

DEAR INSPECTOR,
HAVE YOU BEEN TO THE CINEMA LATELY?

SOMEHOW I HAVE A FEELING THAT YOU HAVE BUT I REALLY THOUGHT YOU WERE BRIGHTER THAN THAT. THIS TIME I'M GOING TO MAKE IT REALLY EASY FOR YOU BY GIVING YOU THREE DAYS. RENDEZVOUS-VOUS ON APRIL 22ND AT 11AM. CAN'T BANK ON MAKING MONEY THESE DAYS. ONE MORE LETTER TO COME. GUY FAWKES

Ashcroft wondered why this man had chosen to write to him directly, why he seemed to be taunting him personally with his impossible clues. He recalled a phrase, a threat, from the first letter, 'Things will get bigger and better'. It would be dangerous to ignore the obvious implication of 'Can't bank on making money'. Indeed the writer's pleasure this time might well be in the knowledge that it would be impossible to protect all the banks in London. Should he confine himself to the major ones? Just those in the City? Their branches in Central London? The whole of Greater London? And what about the Bank of England itself? It was difficult to know where to begin and this time he knew he would have to ask for support from local police forces. He had three days to work in and fully realised what a formidable opponent he was now up against.

Ashcroft had a memorandum printed and distributed to every bank and subsidiary branch in London warning them to be particularly vigilant for the rest of that week and especially on the 22nd because of a security scare. He gave them what little information he could and thought about having a message broadcast on radio and television but decided against this as he didn't want to alarm the population.

He mobilised every available detective and uniformed policeman, cancelled leave and drafted in hundreds of extras from nearby forces for Friday, April 22nd. But what could he tell them to do? Patrol the streets in the vicinity of the banks; circulate among customers; consult with managers and cashiers; search vaults and strong-rooms. There was a robust, visible police presence in and around the Bank of England with armed officers patrolling the streets. Ashcroft checked that all units were in position and told his driver to park down a side street near St Paul's. The seconds ticked by inexorably and 11 o'clock resounded on a nearby church tower.

Almost simultaneously a voice called over the intercom, the message coming through loud and clear. The driver switched on the siren as he screeched away towards the City. The words 'Stock Exchange' hung in the air and, with the wisdom of hindsight, Ashcroft blamed himself for not concentrating more resources there. He took a deep breath as if to summon up the last reserves of strength he needed to face the carnage he expected to find.

The explosion had occurred on the trading floor at the height of the morning's activity. Three people had been killed and many more were seriously injured. Pieces of an old leather briefcase were found, together with the remnants of a detonator and an alarm-clock mechanism identical to those used in the previous incidents. The Stock Exchange was cordoned off, identities were checked and debris was taken to Scotland Yard for analysis. But all these steps proved to be fruitless and the experts could tell Ashcroft nothing that would really help him. Even the clocks failed to produce any useful information; this particular model had been widely sold all over the country for a number of years. He still had nothing to go on: no fingerprints, no identifiable DNA and no notion of where the final strike might be.

The last letter was like the others and, like them, contained no trace of fingerprints. It reached the Inspector's desk on May 3rd.

DEAR INSPECTOR,
BOUGHT ANY GOOD SHARES LATELY? NOW COMES THE BIGGEST AND BEST BANG OF ALL. IT WILL ALSO BE THE LAST AND THE MOST SPECTACULAR. I'M GOING TO GIVE YOU A REAL CHANCE THIS TIME. YOU'VE GOT FOUR DAYS TO THINK ABOUT IT. THE FINAL BANG IS FOR SATURDAY AT 3 O'CLOCK AND WILL HAVE A NATIONAL IMPACT. I ADVISE YOU TO BE IN YOUR OFFICE AT 2PM ON THAT DAY FOR FURTHER INSTRUCTIONS. THE FINAL BANG IS NEARER THAN YOU THINK. **G**UY **F**AWKES

When Ashcroft saw the date two things immediately sprung to mind: firstly there was the FA Cup Final, the biggest sporting event on the English calendar, to be attended by several members of the Royal Family; then there was the state visit of the French President and on Saturday afternoon he was due to visit Downing Street. By an odd and sinister coincidence, both events were scheduled to start at 3 o'clock. It shouldn't be too difficult to ensure the President's safety as routine security measures could easily be stepped up, but the Cup Final . . . . over 90,000 people! Did the word 'Final' bang have any significance? Or did he associate Downing Street and the Prime Minister with Parliament? He was, after all, using the name 'Guy Fawkes' and Parliament was what the original Guy Fawkes had intended to blow up. Then there were all the other national landmarks to be considered.

Could the Royal Family be persuaded not to go to the match? Impossible! It was not uncommon for them to receive threats on their lives and this wasn't even a direct threat. Ashcroft had covered football matches before and shuddered at the thought of all those frenzied supporters. He started making mental notes for the protection of Wembley Stadium but realised that it was just as likely for Guy Fawkes to identify himself with Parliament. Each event represented a potential target.

He wondered why he had been told to be in his office at 2 o'clock; he would have to wait for the answer to that but he had every intention of being there.

During the next three days Ashcroft made what arrangements he could but he was painfully aware of just how inadequate they were likely to be. He went over them countless times with his officers and they in turn briefed and re-briefed their men. He left a colleague to cover Downing Street while he himself concentrated on the Cup Final. The chances of avoiding a catastrophe, however, seemed to diminish with every passing hour.

At 6 o'clock on Saturday morning Inspector Ashcroft was seated at his desk with the Guy Fawkes letter in front of him. He didn't need to read it anymore; he knew it by heart. When his men left for Wembley he slumped down in his chair and was lost in thought. His drawn features emphasised the shadows under his eyes that were bloodshot from lack of sleep. He thought how distant his fishing trip now seemed to be and how desperately he needed to get away. He looked at his watch: 7h45.

His morning was spent checking every detail of the operation several times, conferring again with other senior officers and drinking large quantities of coffee. He had done everything he possibly could to avert the impending disaster but he knew only too well the extent of his helplessness. At 2 o'clock precisely his phone rang and brought his dreadful vigil to an end. His technical staff prepared to trace the incoming call as he picked up the receiver.

"Is that Inspector Ashcroft I have the pleasure of speaking to?"

"It is."

"Inspector William Ashcroft of the CID?"

"Yes."

"Well, well, well! You got my last letter, I presume?"

"Yes, I did."

"Did you notice how it was signed?"

"Of course I did. 'Guy Fawkes' like the others."

"No, Inspector, not quite like the others. Take another look. More closely this time. Look carefully

45

at the signature, at the G and the F. Come on; it seems as if you've missed a big clue there."

"Well, they appear to be written in bold, if that's what you mean."

"Now you've got it. Only the 'G' and the 'F'." Think now. 'GF'. . . . 'GF'. Who do you know with those initials? Don't they mean anything to you? 15 years ago? Your first big case, if I'm not mistaken. See what I mean?"

"Fenton!"

"That's right! You've got it. Gerry Fenton. And before you ask, I'm calling you from right here in Scotland Yard."

The heavy silence that followed sent a shiver down Ashcroft's back.

"You fool, Fenton. Where exactly are you and what do you expect to get out of this? Haven't you done enough damage already? You can't possibly get away with it, you know."

"Oh, I know that. But just think of the satisfaction, revenge, call it what you like."

"What are you here for anyway?"

"Well, certainly not to give myself up if that's what you're thinking. Oh no. I'm in room 27a in the basement of the Yard and you'd better listen very carefully to what I'm saying. You're going to come down here right now so that we can have a little chat. But don't come into the room! There's a flask of nitroglycerin delicately balanced just inside the door and if you try to open it you'll know what to expect. We'll come to that part later. Come on down now. I'll be waiting for you. I'll give you five minutes."

The line went dead before Ashcroft could say another word. Simultaneously a technician knocked and entered his office in a single movement. "He's right here, Sir, in the building." Ashcroft nodded and slowly replaced the receiver. He hung his head in thought.

Fenton was right: it had been his first big case, the first time he had felt personally responsible for such a long sentence being pronounced on a prisoner in the dock. This particular prisoner had taken part in an armed robbery on a warehouse in the East End. His job had been to blow the safe but he had been surprised by a security guard whom he had then proceeded to shoot in the chest. Though sentenced to life imprisonment, he had recently benefited from a parole hearing and was now out again.

Situated at the end of a long corridor, 27a was one of a number of disused storage rooms. Ashcroft and Hurley stopped a few feet from the door and the Inspector wiped a trickle of sweat from his brow. Then he said in a loud voice: "I'm here, Fenton. What do you want me to do? Why don't you think for a moment and just come out? It's your only chance."

A sinister laugh came from inside the room. It was followed by a short silence before Fenton spoke threateningly, "No way, Ashcroft. Now you just listen to me. I'll do the talking. I'm going to tell you all about the final bang because it is the last one and it concerns you personally. It's because of you that I was put inside years ago. You ruined my life and now you're going to pay for it. I've never forgotten that supercilious look you had on your face in court and now I'm going to wipe it off for good."

"Don't be a fool," said the Inspector. "You know you won't be able to get away with this. You can't possibly get out of here."

"Oh, I know that, but I've already taken out one copper and now I'm going for the big one. They'll never get me though. I'm not going behind a bloody cell wall again."

"What do you mean by that?"

"It's very simple really. I've got enough explosives and nitro in here to blow up half of Scotland Yard. I'll be going with you."

Ashcroft was aware of a nauseous feeling in his stomach. He knew that this was not bluff. He heard Fenton's malicious chuckle again and tried to intervene. "Wait a minute, Fenton," he began.

"I'll do better than that," retorted Fenton. "I'll wait the best part of an hour. I want you to have time to think, just like I've had to for 15 years. You'll know when your time is up because I've set an alarm; you'll hear it go off at 3 o'clock and that's when I'm going to throw a little switch here. One little switch, one very big bang. That's when the fun starts! And remember one thing, Ashcroft; don't try to get away. If I think you're creeping off, I'll do it straightaway." There was a moment's pause. Then Fenton added deliberately: "At most, that gives you another fifty-one minutes."

Rooms 27a and 27b had adjacent doors that formed the bottom arm of the letter E which was itself separated from the rest of the basement by a long corridor. The door to 27a was slightly ajar and they could hear Fenton quite clearly. Sergeant Hurley had just been into 27b and, as he came out, he made a reassuring gesture to Ashcroft. Then he went upstairs again. He returned a few minutes later carrying notepads and pencils and was accompanied by several more colleagues. It was clear that any plans they wanted to make, any words they wanted to exchange, would have to be done in silence. The Inspector scribbled a note ordering the total evacuation of Scotland Yard and the clearing of the immediate vicinity. He handed this to one of the policemen, removed his jacket and loosened his tie. It was two thirty-six.

Although there was only one door into 27a and no windows, it had a small ventilation grille, placed high up in the wall that was common to both rooms. Through this, Hurley, by standing on a small table, had been able to see Fenton; he was sitting on some folding steps directly opposite the door. In front of him was a small table on which he had assembled a complicated-looking contraption of wires, cylinders and switches, together with a simple alarm clock. Although several small bottles and a flask were also visible, there might well have been more as most of the room was hidden from view by deep racks of dusty files.

It was vital to keep him talking, to keep him occupied and, above all, unsuspecting. It was not easy to do this and, at the same time, make the desperate plans that might just prevent a disaster.

"Listen Fenton," said the Inspector. "You're a sick man. You can't be judged in your present condition. We'll get you medical help. I can promise you that."

Fenton's sneering reaction showed what he thought of that offer. He wasn't going to be tricked into anything.

49

Ashcroft was at a loss. He felt helpless. He must try to assemble his thoughts. He would appeal to Fenton's ego: "Tell me, Fenton. How did someone like you get into Scotland Yard in the first place?"

"Nothing simpler. I saw some electricians coming in here last week. They told me they were re-wiring the basement and that they would be here for a couple more weeks so I picked up a false identity card from a mate of mine, got chatting to your doorman and made a number of visits down here. No one was going to suspect an electrician carrying coils of wire and a toolbox. The nitro was a bit more tricky but it's surprising what you can do with an old lunch flask. They let me in this morning when I told them we had a problem and that I had to do some overtime. I've got enough equipment down here now to make a pretty mess of things."

As Fenton detailed the explosives he had in place, Ashcroft made brief comments to show that he was still there while he and Hurley hurriedly examined every course of action open to them. They couldn't use force because of the nitro behind the door and elsewhere. They couldn't pipe gas through the vent as Fenton would smell it before it took effect. A stun grenade was no use for obvious reasons. They couldn't hope to make him change his mind - he already had too much to answer for. There was only one solution and it was drastic but there was no alternative. He had to be taken out, neutralised.

Sergeant Hurley scribbled a quick note to Ashcroft who nodded his approval. He then went back along the corridor and returned five minutes later carrying a rifle. Among his numerous accomplishments, he was a member of a special intervention team in which he was an elite marksman. He had also represented Great Britain in international firearms competitions on a number of occasions. He exchanged glances with Ashcroft who again nodded his agreement. It was ten to three.

Hurley returned to room 27b and hopped nimbly up on the table in the corner of the room. He had an excellent view of Fenton through the ventilation panel. What he saw was a ferrety little creature sitting on the steps, holding an ominous-looking bottle. He could also see an array of deadly-looking equipment as well as several more bottles and a flask, all strategically placed around the room. Fenton's eyes burned with the fire of pent-up rage. The Sergeant shouldered the rifle, looked through the sights and held Fenton in the crosshairs. He couldn't fire the shot that would bring them all relief, however, as Fenton was still holding a bottle of clear liquid. Hurley held his breath, watched, waited, understood the role he played, realised the price of failure.

With two and a half minutes left and to show he was still outside 27a, Ashcroft spoke again. In this last desperate exchange he tried pleading, threatening, cajoling, even flattering him for his bomb-making prowess – all to no avail, as he knew it would be. Fenton's mind was made up and there was no way anyone was going to change it.

Ashcroft was rebuffed for the final time and, instead of persuading Fenton to cooperate, he was ordered to join him in the final countdown. "40. . . . 39. . . . 38. . . . 37. . . . "

With 12 seconds remaining on the clock Fenton carefully replaced the bottle on the table and turned his attention to the apparatus. His finger hovered above the switch that he obviously intended to press. The Inspector counted mechanically, all the time waiting for his world to collapse around him, for the searing flash that would blast him into oblivion. "10. . . . 9. . . . 8. . . . 7. . . . "

Sergeant Hurley watched Fenton through the grille, saw him place the bottle on the table, realised that this was his window of opportunity. He braced himself for what he knew he had to do and, as Fenton straightened up, he seized the moment and pulled the trigger.

Ashcroft heard the crack of the rifle being fired, held his breath, bowed his head.

Nothing happened.

There was no explosion.

Fenton's body twitched and his eyes rolled up. He threw his hands in the air and swayed for a moment on the steps before falling heavily to his left. He didn't move again.

Ashcroft felt no elation, just an intense feeling of relief. He closed his eyes and exhaled profoundly, oblivious to the ringing of a cheap alarm-clock on the other side of the door.

It didn't take the bomb squad long to gain access into 27a and defuse the deadly devices that Fenton had assembled.

Two hours later Dr Patterson joined the others in Ashcroft's office. He had come straight from the Yard's laboratories where he had just completed his initial analysis. He was carrying a sheet of metal and a pipette containing a small amount of yellowish liquid. "You know, Bill, you're a lucky man to be still with us. That fellow wasn't bluffing." He placed the metal sheet on the floor, squeezed the little rubber bulb on the end of the pipette and released a single drop of nitroglycerin. The ensuing detonation was felt by everyone in the room and Ashcroft, who was sitting on the corner of his desk, jumped visibly, knocking off a sheet of paper. As he stooped to pick it up, his eye fell on the bottom line: THE FINAL BANG IS NEARER THAN YOU THINK.

How right Guy Fawkes had been.

HALF THE HOUSE

Harry and Marjorie had married much later than the average couple. Both in their late 50's, they were rather set in their respective ways and, although they knew marriage was supposed to be something of a compromise, each of them was very determined and a little headstrong. They had both built up a considerable amount of money and had pooled their resources to purchase a small house, without needing to arrange a mortgage. The deeds to the house were registered jointly in their two names.

As they settled down to married life, they thought the advantages of a shared existence generally outweighed the inconveniences, and they developed a genuine fondness for each other. Nevertheless they liked to maintain a certain sense of independence and to feel that they were making their own decisions; this had long been their way of life and was something they jealously sought to maintain.

They had strong opinions on most matters and used to react forcefully, even vehemently, to what they read in the papers or saw on television. They were interested in, but sceptical of, the media generally. While considering an article or awaiting the outcome of a particular situation, they would often express impassioned reactions and leave no doubt as to where they stood. "I'd bet the house on that one," became a standard response to show total conviction on a given matter; "I'd put half the house on that," when there was still some doubt; or again, "Well, my half of the house, in any case," when they had clearly divergent views. When one of them felt less than fully convinced, that would become, "Well, YOUR half of the house, anyway."

The "half the house" idea really took hold and soon became an integral part of their conversations, but over time it became more than that. Although they genuinely loved each other, they were still very jealous of what some people might refer to as "one's own space," and, as the years went by, they had each developed little habits and idiosyncrasies that the other found annoying. Harry chomped on his food, got up at 5h30 every day and sometimes left dirty clothes on the bedroom floor. Marjorie walked round the house in hair curlers, had a habit of creeping up unnoticed and liked soap operas. Sometimes they actually seemed to be looking for things to complain about.

Then, with the passing of time, "my half of the house" became more territorial and proprietorial. Marjorie didn't want Harry in the kitchen anymore and she wasn't welcome in the garage. Each one acceded to the desires of the other but the situation continued to deteriorate until they finally sat down for a serious discussion on the matter. This lasted for two hours with a limited amount of give and take on both sides. In the end they agreed to live on as a partnership, share their lives and even do some things together but, at the same time, retain a certain measure of independence. There was no question of separation and certainly not of divorce. They drew up a private contract, wrote it out on the computer, printed two copies and signed them. It stated that they were still very fond of each other but that, henceforth, they agreed to stick to their designated areas of the house. So they decided to set about determining just what these 'designated areas' were to be.

The bedrooms posed no problem are there were just two. Marjorie claimed the upstairs bathroom while Harry agreed the downstairs shower room/toilet would be enough for him. In exchange for the kitchen, Harry obtained the garage and dining room where it was agreed that meals were to be served for both of them. As there was only one lounge, their solution was to use it on alternate days. The only remaining area was the garden and this was declared to be open territory to be enjoyed jointly or individually, as desired. Harry said he would see to its upkeep.

They also agreed to have individual housework responsibilities. Marjorie said she would do the shopping and cooking for both of them if Harry agreed to do the washing up and rubbish disposal for which he would be allowed into the kitchen. She added that she would take on the clothes washing as well if Harry cleaned the house and did the ironing.

Once again they agreed on this but, when she saw his initial attempt to iron one of her favourite blouses, she quickly took over that role too.

They still came together to watch the occasional TV programme or to listen to a concert but that didn't work out too well sometimes and the accusations started to fly:

"I found two spiders in my bathroom last week!" she whined.

"You served me broccoli 3 days running!" he retorted.

"You spilled water on the kitchen floor twice in two days!"

"There was none of my toothpaste left this morning!"

Despite their differences, they co-inhabited in this way for several years. The one thing they always seemed to agree on was that there was still something not quite right about the way they lived.

As the atmosphere became more tense they had another of their long discussions, managed not to argue too much and came to the reluctant conclusion that perhaps they should sell the house and each one buy a separate abode. They called in an estate agent, explained the situation to him and, surprisingly, quickly agreed on a selling price for their house. He, in turn, had a proposition for them; he could offer them a house, not too far away, that had been beautifully converted into two separate and independent apartments 5 years before. They liked the idea, agreed in principle on a price, visited the property, accepted the estate agent as arbiter and said they would buy them, naturally with two distinct sets

57

of deeds. The change-over would take a week which they would spend in the Hotel Splendid, in separate rooms, of course.

Two years after moving in, they celebrated 15 years of marriage, if indeed not exactly of wedded bliss, by going to a pleasant little restaurant in the nearby town for dinner. Physically, of course, they had changed over the years; both were somewhat greyer, he was more stooped and a little thinner and she had visibly put on the kilos. They enjoyed their meal together and chatted amicably throughout. When they returned home, Marjorie invited Harry into her apartment for a cup of coffee and there they talked for another two hours.

She admitted that she didn't really enjoy washing up too much and Harry thought his cooking and poor diet were causing him to lose weight. Their discussion continued on until nearly midnight when they reluctantly went their separate ways.

One balmy afternoon within the week an observant passer-by might have noticed them sitting in the garden with a stranger they had just met. As they sipped their fruit juice and nibbled on a piece of home-baked fruitcake, Harry turned to their visitor and said tentatively but with a certain conviction, "Now, Mr Wilkins, you're a distinguished architect. As you know, this house was originally built as a one-family dwelling place. We've asked you to come round this afternoon to tell us the feasibility and approximate cost of putting in a wooden staircase and converting it back into a single accommodation."

All the while Marjorie had been nodding her head in acquiescence. Then she smiled at Harry, turned back to Mr Wilkins and said emphatically. "And let's be clear about one thing. We would, of course, want the deeds to be drawn up so that the house would be jointly in both our names."

NUMBER NINE

Billy Mason was easily recognisable. He was blond haired, 21 years old, handsome and muscular, and he had the most engaging smile. Among sports fans he was practically a household name. He was now on the fringes of the England football team and all the experts thought he would represent his country within the year. His ambition was to help them retain the World Cup which they had won two years before. The whole country was gripped by football fever and competition for a place in the national team was intense.

Billy played for the Rovers in the First Division. They did have a more complete and formal name but, as they had been one of the top four teams for about ten years now, everyone, including their rivals, simply referred to them as 'The Rovers'. Billy had first joined them four years before when a scout had spotted him playing for his school team and signed him up as an apprentice within the week. 1966 had been a great year for English football and for Billy. England won the World Cup and, at 18, Billy made his first team debut for the Rovers at centre forward.

Now, in 1968, he commanded a regular first team place, had played for England Under 21's and had been named in the national squad for the next senior game. He was going from strength to strength and frequently took pride of place in the sports pages.

Just before Christmas on a slippery, rain-drenched pitch, Rovers were playing at home against their fiercest rivals in a vital match. Towards the end of the game they were drawing 1-1 in front of 63,000 spectators. As usual, Billy was proudly wearing the centre forward's number 9 shirt. One of his defenders skilfully slipped the ball through to him and he sprinted forward to latch onto the pass. The opposing full back came across and kicked out at the ball but Billy jinked and turned, setting up the perfect scoring opportunity. He shaped up to strike the ball, eyed the corner of the goal he was going to aim at and drew back his leg to shoot. At that precise moment the other full back came sliding across the greasy surface, lunged out at the ball, missed it, crashed into Billy and landed with his full weight on Billy's leg.

Billy went down in a heap, heard the bone snap and felt the unbearable pain shoot through his leg. He lay there, semi-conscious, until the medical team had splinted his leg. Then he was removed on a stretcher, put in an ambulance and taken to hospital. The news could not have been worse; in addition to a shattered tibia, he had sustained torn ligaments and a ruptured meniscus. Two days later he underwent lengthy surgery and started his long convalescence. After a month, the doctors told him he would never play again.

In a matter of moments that fateful Saturday his whole life had changed. Instead of the smiling, happy-go-lucky young man he had been, he became despondent, introverted, bad tempered and bitter. Though they well understood the reason for this change in him, his team mates and friends found it difficult to be in his company for any length of time and started to see him less and less frequently. He didn't even go to the Rovers games any more. The club in turn seemed to turn away from him and before long he hardly saw anyone and just wanted to be alone.

In his carefree playing days he had been paid very good wages for someone so young but with partying, girls and hangers-on he had not really saved anything substantial. Neither had he taken out any meaningful insurance coverage. So, at the age of 21, he had no job, no prospects, nothing to look forward to. His parents had emigrated to Canada three years before and he had no desire to follow them there. He could just afford to rent a dingy 4th floor apartment in a seedy graffiti-daubed building and became something of a recluse. He had received a small compensation package after his accident and had put it towards a second-hand car but he rarely wanted to go anywhere and the running costs did not justify keeping it so he sold it on at a loss. Thereafter he took a variety of menial jobs to ensure some kind of income and, at different times, he packed shelves in a supermarket, washed cars and even sold newspapers. Nobody he worked with recognised him and wherever he went he was viewed as a sad loner. His needs were few, just the bare essentials, and basically he found he could manage on social benefits.

1998. 30 years have passed. A generation. But not much has changed for Billy. Same apartment, very little human contact, no real friends, no hint of a smile. He had, of course aged: thinning hair, blond streaked with grey, lined face, the suggestion of a stoop and a permanent heavy limp. He had spent his 50th birthday alone, still in the same apartment. For a while now there had been talk of demolishing Billy's block of flats. He had no idea what he would do if that happened but finally the owners decided to refurbish it instead. Perhaps out of sheer relief, Billy, in turn, redecorated his own place and painted it in brighter colours. He must have felt pleased with the result but his deadpan expression gave no hint to this effect and he continued to view the world through a pair of mournful eyes.

Over the years his next-door neighbours had come and gone and now a lady in her early 60's lived there. She seemed pleasant enough but they barely exchanged the time of day when they crossed each other in the corridor. Several times he had seen her with a young boy who appeared to be her grandson. Each time the boy had been carrying a football which he cradled fondly under his arm. Then, one day, out of curiosity, having passed them on the stairs, Billy looked out of the window to see what they were doing. Down below in the public park, he saw the two of them, about 20 metres apart, kicking the ball to one another. The elderly lady was not too accurate but the boy seemed to caress the ball and place it exactly where he wanted it. Billy was intrigued.

Next day he saw the two of them in the corridor again, clearly on their way down for a kickabout. He took his courage in both hands, "Do you mind if I ask you something?" he said. "If you like, I could go down and kick around with the lad."

The lady looked relieved, smiled and said, "Really? Thank you very much. I'm afraid I'm not very good at football."

They exchanged a few niceties and Billy discovered that the boy's name was Jamie, that he was 10 years old, that his mother worked in a supermarket and that Grandma took him for a couple of hours each day after school. He later found out that there was no father; he had abandoned the family when Jamie was still a baby. After their session together, they returned to their respective apartments, Billy having asked if he might do the same thing the following day. And so the habit developed.

Usually it was Jamie who came knocking at the door to get things started but it must be admitted that Billy always sat there waiting to be summoned. He could see that the boy was a natural and realised that just kicking the ball backwards and forwards to one another was a waste of time and talent. So he began to organise training sessions and taught Jamie all the essential skills a good footballer needs. He taught him to shoot, to dribble, to pass the ball accurately, to feint, to head, to trap the ball and to hit a volley and a half-volley. They practised speed off the mark, quick turns, sprinting, endurance running and, especially, the importance of being able to use both feet. This went on for six months or so until their sessions were interrupted by the summer holidays.

During the next couple of years their relationship changed, too. In the circumstances there was little more Billy could do for Jamie but he felt immensely proud of what they had achieved together. The boy went on to secondary school, got into the school team and played regularly with a group of friends on the nearby common. On the other hand, he still visited his grandmother several times a week and on those occasions he liked to call in and see Billy for a chat. Billy told him why he still had a serious limp and from there they went on to talk about his incredible but short-lived career, the Rovers and some of his most spectacular goals. They spoke about the great strikers of that era, Nat Lofthouse, Bobby Charlton, Geoff Hurst, George Best and many more, and also about the honour and responsibility of wearing the mythical number 9 shirt. All the while, Billy still retained that melancholy, far-away look that had become so characteristic of him.

Like so many people before her, Jamie's grandmother left the neighbourhood and Jamie didn't call in any more. Every Saturday morning Billy went to watch the school matches and, the following year, the representative side that Jamie played for. After each game they got together for a while and analysed Jamie's performance. The learning curve continued and he was then selected for the County under 15's. Billy took great pride in Jamie's progress but he kept it to himself. He rarely said much except to explain what he wanted the boy to do. This was no problem for Jamie; they didn't need to speak; they had a tacit understanding, a silent complicity, their own way of communicating.

Billy's mind was made up. He thought the lad was ready to face up to the rigours and challenges of the big time. A former team-mate of his, Harry Kendall, was often mentioned in the media as being the Chief Scout for the Rovers and he decided to approach the subject with him. After three days of trying to see him, he spotted him getting into his black BMW 7 Series in the club car park late one afternoon. As the car approached the automatic barrier, he waved it down and went up to the driver's window. After some hesitation, Kendall recognised him and invited him to get into the car. They drove off and stopped at a nearby cafe for a drink and a chat. Billy explained the whole situation to him and Kendall agreed, 'for old time's sake,' to take a look at Jamie.

The young footballer turned up one morning at the Rovers training complex and was introduced to Martin Fraser, the assistant manager who, after a brief conversation, sent him to see the youth team coach. He was invited to come back each day for a fortnight and was then sent back to see Fraser who told him that Rovers were prepared to offer him a contract as an apprentice. He was completely overjoyed as he had always dreamed of one day playing for them. On the way home he called in to see Billy and they talked and drank fruit juice together for more than an hour.

From there on Jamie's progression was truly remarkable. He impressed everyone at the club, trained like one possessed, developed his innate skills and, on his 16th birthday, was invited to sign professional forms. He soon got into the reserve team, playing regularly for them for two years and continuing to learn his trade. And then, with the start of the new season in 2006, his big moment arrived. Billy had sensed that he was not far from making a break-through and had started buying several newspapers every morning looking for news of the boy prodigy. His reward came in August when he read the following headline in a national newspaper: 'Jamie Marshall Makes the Grade. 18 year Old Will Debut for Rovers at the Weekend.'

Billy followed his meteoric rise throughout the season in the papers and on TV. He was scoring goals regularly, frequently making the headlines and becoming a star in his own right. Not surprisingly they lost contact as Jamie's existence was taken up with games, training sessions, interviews, the media, publicity, sponsorship, cars, girls and the numerous other demands made on a professional footballer. Over the next two years he established himself as the automatic choice for centre forward and was consistently the club's leading goal scorer.

One morning in September, 2009, Billy awoke early as he usually did, got up, dressed and went out to buy the papers. He went into the local cafe and ordered a coffee, sat down near a window, picked up the first paper and turned to the back page. The headline and lead article were about the upcoming international against Germany. The starting line-up was spelled out in large characters in a separate column and, as Billy glanced down the list of names, his heart missed a beat as he read, 'Centre forward, Number 9, Jamie Marshall'. He ordered a second cup of coffee, must have read the papers at least a dozen times and just sat there dreaming. As soon as he got back to his apartment he sat down at the kitchen table and wrote a letter:

Dear Jamie,

I hope you still remember me. I have followed your progress with great interest and want to congratulate you on being selected to represent England. I always knew you had it in you. I'll be watching the game on TV and following your every move. Crack a couple in for me. Enjoy the whole experience. You certainly deserve it. With best wishes and good luck.
From your friend,
Billy Mason.

He addressed the letter to "Jamie Marshall, c/o The Rovers Football Club," went straight out to catch the morning post and hoped it would find him safely.

Billy slept very well that night. At 11 o'clock the following morning there was a knock on his door. He opened it and could hardly believe the sight that greeted him. There, with a broad smile on his face, stood Jamie. They shook hands warmly.

"Jamie!" he gasped, "What a surprise. Come in. Come on in."

"Hello, Billy. It's good to see you again. I've been a bit busy recently but I've got the morning off today so I thought I'd drop in and see you. By the way, thanks for your letter."

"It was nothing. I'm just glad I had the chance to write that one. Come in. Come in."

Billy produced a carton of fruit juice and a couple of glasses and they sat down at the table, smiling and enjoying each other's company. After a moment or two, Jamie put his hand in his pocket. "I thought you might like to have this," he said, proffering a buff-coloured envelope. "Here, open it."

Billy opened the flap and withdrew the contents, the latest generation Rovers necktie.

"That's great, Jamie. Thank you. I'll wear it with pride."

"There's something else in there, too," said the young star.

Billy looked inside again and pulled out a smaller envelope. His quizzical expression vanished as he discovered that it contained a ticket for the Germany game.

"I thought it would be better to watch it live," said Jamie.

Billy couldn't express his feelings but he didn't have to; Jamie understood.

As he sipped his orange juice, Jamie noticed a morning paper on top of some books at the end of the table. When he picked it up to glance at the headlines, he saw what it had concealed: two large format scrapbooks. With a picture of Jamie himself gracing the top cover, it was very clear what that book was likely to contain. Billy explained that he had enjoyed following his progress for the last few years and that he had wanted to keep a record of it. Jamie flipped through the pages and, stretching out to put it back, was intrigued by the second book. It was a well-thumbed volume with a rather grainy black and white newspaper cutting on the cover. It featured Billy himself scoring what was generally considered to have been his greatest goal. The book reviewed the whole of his illustrious but all-too-short career and they spent half an hour going through the old clippings, programmes and other memorabilia.

All too soon Jamie said he had to leave, and together they stood up and walked to the door. "Just a second, before you go," said Billy and he turned away and went to a cupboard in the corner of the room before returning to Jamie carrying a flat cardboard box. "This is for you. Please take it." Jamie placed it on the table, removed the lid and withdrew a neatly-folded, old-style football shirt. "That's the one I wore for my first Rovers game," said Billy proudly.

With a lump in his throat, Jamie thanked him and made his way towards the door. Then he paused, turned round and looked into Billy's eyes. The two men shared a long, intense embrace and Jamie was gone.

That Saturday Billy was at Wembley Stadium several hours before kick-off time. He went to his allocated seat as soon as the gates opened and found that he was in a prime location on the halfway line. He enjoyed the buildup to the match and, though showing no visible sign of emotion, he was inwardly excited as the two teams were led out and lined up in the centre of the pitch. After the national anthems had been played, the players faced the main stand and waved to the crowd. Billy saw only one face, the one that was looking directly up at him. As they turned to salute the other side, they presented their backs to Billy and the only thing he could see was a shirt bearing the name 'Marshall' and a large and gratifying number 9.

At that moment Billy drew a deep breath, put his head back and allowed himself a discreet smile. Two warm tears welled out of his eyes, trickled down his face and splashed on to the programme he was holding.

At least one of his dreams had come true.

BORDER CROSSING

The tatty, dog-eared identity card bore the name 'Juan Pietro Carlos Antonio Perez' but, as he handed it over to the customs officer, the little man whose face it bore grinned up at him and said, "But you can call me Chico."

"I'm the Jefe round these parts," replied the burly officer as he ostentatiously stroked the stripes on the sleeve of his uniform. "And this is Pablo."

Chico was a small, wiry individual in his early 50's. Despite a considerable number of missing teeth, he had an engaging smile and appeared to have the personality to go with it. He certainly made an impression on the Jefe whose fleeting smile revealed a flash of gold-capped teeth and whose heavy breath betrayed more than a hint of garlic.

The customs post was a little-frequented rural crossing in South America which was nonetheless on the fringes of a large town, "The Big City" as it was familiarly called by the locals. It represented the prosperous side of the border where, it was claimed, there were more cars than mules! And that was where Chico was now heading.

The Jefe returned the card to him and he stuffed it in his shirt pocket, retrieved his bicycle, gave a cheery wave and set off on his journey again. The official looked at his colleague, shrugged his shoulders and chuckled. Then they sat down again to enjoy the warm morning sunshine and watched Chico pedal off into the distance.

The following morning at approximately the same time Chico rode up to the crossing again. The officers recognised him, waved away the ID card he proffered, went back to their office and sipped on some strong black coffee. This happened every day that week and the three of them were striking up a good relationship and were becoming, at least superficially, quite friendly. At the same time there was something about Chico that puzzled the customs men and they were, after all, conscientious professionals.

From the standard questions that they asked, Chico had informed them that he came from a nearby town on the poorer side of the frontier and that he cycled over to the big city each day to visit an elderly aunt of his, to do a little shopping for her and to help her around the house. This was a very laudable explanation but, after another week or two, the officers were beginning to feel really suspicious and thought there must be something else that they ought to know. They checked up on his story, only to discover that his aunt did, in fact, live in the town and that she was in poor health.

One day they saw him in the distance cycling, as usual, in their direction and were surprised to see him stop. He carefully laid his bike down on the ground, took off the haversack he was wearing on his back and sat down in the shade of a tree. He rarely carried a haversack and they thought they were finally on to something.

"Quickly! Fetch the binoculars!" ordered the Jefe. Pablo handed him a pair and took one himself and they carefully trained them on Chico to see what he was going to do next. They brought the lenses into sharp focus and held their breath. Chico slowly unfastened the straps of the haversack, loosened the cord and looked with evident pleasure at the contents. He set the bag down by his side and leaned back against the tree. It was another ten minutes before he again turned his attention to the bag, delicately withdrew an object wrapped in paper and placed it on the ground beside him. But it was still out of sight to the officers. The binoculars positively trembled as they waited for Chico's next move. They didn't have to wait long; Chico turned towards the packet, picked it up, unwrapped it and started to munch on a delicious-looking salami sandwich! When he had finished eating, he crumpled the wrapper, put it back in his rucksack, mounted his bike and carried on cycling towards them.

A number of weeks came and went and the routine remained the same. Then one morning they decided they just had to interrogate him more closely to try to solve their conundrum. They told him to prop his bike up against a nearby wall and go with them to the interview room behind the office. His story remained rigorously the same except for the fact that he said his aunt was growing steadily weaker and was depending on him more and more. He certainly didn't appear to have lost any of his good humour though, nor to resent the fact that he was being interrogated. He was, as usual, polite and deferential.

The customs men, however, were now convinced that Chico must be smuggling something across the border and, seeing this as a challenge, decided to do all they could to prove their case. In the next few weeks they frisked him and did a body search on numerous occasions, looked carefully at the heels of his old shoes, inside his hat band, tried to unscrew his buttons, looked inside his mouth. He must clearly be passing something very small: drugs, precious stones, gold? One day they examined his bike particularly closely: removed the saddle and handlebars, peered inside and reached into the tubes, took the wheels off, removed the chain, handle grips and brakes. All to no avail. Despite their painstaking efforts, they could find nothing.

Chico all the while remained sanguine, continued to smile at them and said he perfectly understood that they had to do their job. Their relationship continued to be friendly and he was still greeted warmly each morning. He bore them no grudge and they found him quite entertaining and even invited him into their office to drink coffee together and discuss cars, women and football.

About six months after he had first crossed the border Chico told them that this was going to be his last week. He reassured them that his dear old aunt was now well on the mend and that there was no need for him to visit her any more on a regular basis. The officers were actually rather sad to hear this and said

75

they would miss him and their friendly discussions together. In any case they had long since given up all hope of ever pinning anything on him. When they learned that Friday would be his last day, they invited him to come a little earlier than usual to share a glass of wine with them. He rode up as requested, propped his bike against the wall and joined them in their little office.

They poured three generous glasses of the local red 'dynamite' and drank a toast before producing some ham and cheese and a loaf of crusty bread. They sat around the little wooden table, three friends enjoying each other's company, nibbling on the victuals and discussing their favourite topics of conversation.

As Chico stood up to take his leave, the Jefe said, "Listen Chico. We all know each other pretty well here, don't we, and I'm going to be perfectly honest with you. For some time now we have both suspected that you must be smuggling something across the border. If so, then just level with us and we promise it won't go any further."

Pablo concurred with a vigorous nodding of his head before adding, "That's right, Chico. You have our word for it. Come on. What is it?"

A sheepish grin passed over Chico's face. He raised his eyebrows, thought for a moment and scratched his head. As he walked towards the door, he stopped, turned round and looked at each of them in turn. Then he grinned again, shrugged his shoulders and said simply, "Bicycles!"

DOWN THE LITTLE LANE

It was just a little cottage in the country but it was our escape, our refuge, our weekend retreat. It was only 30 minutes from our town house but spending a couple of days there at weekends felt like moving into another universe. We just loved it. We, that is myself, my wife, Angela, our two children, Melanie, aged three and her big brother, Michael, six.

The cottage was located up a rudimentary road about one kilometre outside a small village which, in turn, was somewhat isolated from the rest of humanity. We were able to buy it thanks to some money we had inherited from Angela's parents. We had developed the habit of driving there every Friday evening and returning on Sunday afternoon.

On Saturday mornings we nearly always had a visitor; an old man, probably in his early seventies, would come shuffling along the narrow road looking expectantly at our front door. The first time we saw him he just stood there scratching his head and clearly hoping for an invitation to come inside. It would have been churlish not to indulge him.

He was small in stature, somewhat hunched and very wrinkled. His thinning hair was grey turning white and he wore it long. He always carried a couple of days' stubble. His clothes looked old but clean and his overall appearance inspired a certain sympathy for him. To begin with, little Melanie wasn't too sure and clung nervously to her mother's leg.

We invited him to sit down at the table and he gladly accepted to share a glass of wine with us. He stayed for about 30 minutes and during that time we spoke about the weather, the weather and the weather. It was a long half hour and a little embarrassing, punctuated by many silences, but there was something pleasant about his company and we invited him to call in again the following weekend.

He seemed decidedly more relaxed on his second visit. He also stayed a little longer and, in his own laconic style, volunteered some basic information about himself. We discovered that he was called Ernest, had worked most of his life as a farmhand, had been retired for a number of years and had become something of a recluse. He told us that he had his own small cottage further up the hill, among the trees, down an even smaller path. We subsequently learned that his wife had died 10 years previously and that he had no children. He was indeed a man alone.

During subsequent weeks, months and even years, Ernest became a regular Saturday visitor. He always arrived round about noon and we grew to appreciate his company. Even the children lost their inhibitions and by the time they were 8 and 5 they chatted quite happily with him. In fact he seemed to be completely at ease with them and would often draw little sketches for them, a skill for which he appeared to have a real talent.

With us he remained serious and liked to reminisce about his early days. Little by little we built up a picture of the kind of life he had led. He explained that he had left school at the age of 14, joined the Navy and taken part in the Second World War. He didn't want to go into much detail on that subject and we certainly weren't going to press him on it.

He rarely missed a Saturday visit and clearly looked forward to the weekends. Strangely enough, he never wanted to stay and eat with us but it wasn't very difficult to persuade him to take some food away with him and eat it in his own place. Angela always allowed for an extra portion and started to bring ready-meals for him from our main home.

One weekend Michael had mumps and we were unable to go to the cottage. The following Saturday Ernest came down much earlier than usual to see us. At first he seemed to take our previous absence as a personal affront but, on hearing the reason for it, his concern and affection were practically tangible and he insisted on giving both children a big hug.

Though he had been coming to see us for nearly two years, he just suddenly appeared on the road each time, as if falling out of a tree. We had long been torn between discretion and curiosity but our dilemma came to an end one week when Michael suddenly blurted out: "Where exactly do you live then,

Ernest?" Ernest was willing enough to explain and it was Melanie who added, "Can we come and see you there?" He explained that he had a small cottage further up the road, down a little lane, and told us exactly how to get there. "And yes, Melanie," he added, "you certainly can come and see me if you want to." And so it was that next morning we all set off up the road to pay him a visit.

Angela took him a cake she had baked and the children, who by now had grown very fond of him, did some special drawings. After walking for five minutes we found the little lane he had described. It was barely more than a grassy footpath and led us through some thick woodland and into a small clearing in the woods. There, in the middle of it, was Ernest's cottage, a tiny stone-built dwelling like something out of a children's story book. In answer to our knocking on his door Ernest called out, "Come in. It's never locked."

We opened the door and found ourselves in the kitchen which, it soon became apparent, was where Ernest spent most of his time. It contained an old-fashioned sink, a few plates and saucepans on an open shelf, a simple cupboard, an ancient two-ring electric cooker and a small electric heater. There was also an old and battered radio on a simple wooden table and a broom propped up in one corner of the room. There was no television, no books and no other appliances. A creaky armchair completed the furnishings. At the back of the room there were two more doors, presumably leading to a bathroom and a bedroom.

Having enjoyed a glass of home-made fruit juice with him, we were on the point of leaving when Ernest said, "Let me get you a few things to take back to town with you." He took us round to the back of the cottage where we discovered a large and most impressive vegetable patch. He also had some chickens and a few rabbits. We decided he must live mostly on stewed vegetables and eggs.

Time passed. The children were now teenagers and Ernest was well over 80. We still went to the cottage most weekends and received our visitor as usual. Then one Saturday he failed to come down for his weekly chat. We didn't take too much notice and thought we would see him on the Sunday morning instead. But again there was no sign of him. By late afternoon when we were due to leave for home, he still had not appeared. We decided to check on him to make sure he was all right.

So together we walked up the hill, down the little lane and up to Ernest's front door. I knocked. There was no answer. I knocked harder and in reply heard a feeble groaning sound. I pushed the door open but Ernest was nowhere to be seen. I called his name and heard the same moaning noises coming from the back of the cottage. I walked through the kitchen and opened the bedroom door. As I stepped inside the room, two things struck me.

Firstly Ernest himself was lying on a small bed in a corner of the room, his sunken eyes wide open, his head lolling over the side of the bed. He was feverish, breathing rapidly and in a state of delirium. In his confusion he was speaking a kind of gibberish and kept repeating that he wanted to ride his horse to market. Angela, who is a qualified nurse, immediately recognised a case of severe dehydration.

The second thing that met my eyes was truly astonishing and took up the rest of the surprisingly spacious room. It was a veritable artist's studio. In addition to all the usual paraphernalia, folded easels, rows of brushes, multifarious tubes of paint and bottles of cleansing fluid, there was row upon row of completed works. At a glance I reckoned there must have been at least 200.

The urgency of the moment necessitated the immediate summoning of an ambulance. Given her professional experience, I left that responsibility to Angela. She quickly transmitted the relevant information and was told that an ambulance should be with us within twenty minutes. Meanwhile she did what she could to calm Ernest and make him as comfortable as possible. When the ambulance arrived, the paramedics inserted a drip in his arm, did a few basic tests and set out on the return journey. Soon he was comfortably installed in a hospital bed and doctors confirmed that he was indeed suffering from dehydration. It was only when I went to the administrative offices to register his entry that I realised we didn't even know his family name.

The hospital, of course, also took my details and contacted me after a few days when Ernest had sufficiently recovered to be discharged. We asked him to stay with us for a while but, not surprisingly, he said he wanted to go home. We drove him back to his cottage and saw to it that he was safely ensconced once more. We also fixed him up with a supply of food for the week and made sure that he had plenty of liquid reserves. The door at the back of the kitchen was still open and together we entered his bedroom/studio. Though reluctant to talk about himself, I could see that he felt he owed us some sort of explanation.

"It's just a hobby," he began. "I've had it for a long time now, especially since I stopped work. I just do it for fun really. It's something I've always enjoyed. Have a look round if you like." We did, and were astonished at both the number and variety of his works. There were landscapes, seascapes, portraits and even abstracts, all neatly arranged in different categories.

"I'd like you to choose one that appeals to you and keep it," he said coyly. "That is if you can find one you like."

That didn't take long as we spotted a self-portrait that had obviously been done fairly recently.

"How about this one, Ernest? Would that be OK?"

"Of course," he replied. "I'd like that."

The portrait in question now enjoys pride-of-place on the wall in our lounge and we have arranged for the County Art Gallery to exhibit a selection of his landscapes.

We continued to spend time in our cottage more or less regularly and, naturally, to see Ernest each time we went there but the children now had other teenage interests and accompanied us less and less frequently. Three years after the hospital episode, when Michael left school and with great regret, we found we had to sell up our second home to help finance his university education. Before doing so, we arranged to have a box of groceries delivered regularly to Ernest and for a social worker to call in on him once a week. We still went to see him occasionally.

More years slipped by. Michael was married and had a three year old daughter, Melanie was finishing university, I was looking forward to retiring and Ernest had turned 90. The occasion called for a celebration and, if not a party, then at least a visit. We packed the car with various types of food and drink, a warm sweater, an extensive selection of oil paints and, of course, a bottle of champagne. We found him in excellent spirits.

It was a bit of a squeeze for six of us plus young Chloe to fit in his kitchen but he was particularly thrilled to meet our little grandchild. He took her on his knee at the table and sketched a clown riding on an elephant for her. She chuckled with delight at the result.

We spent a most enjoyable afternoon together but all too soon it was time to go home. Everyone felt a little sad to leave but Ernest suddenly raised a finger in the air and his eyes lit up: "Ah! I've just had an idea," he said, sitting down behind his easel. "I think you're going to like this one." And he immediately set to work. He looked up as we exited the cottage, waved in our general direction and added a cheery, "Bye. See you next time!"

The 'next time' came sooner than any of us would have expected. Ten days later we received a phone call from the social worker who visited him, informing us that Ernest had died. She had found him slumped over at his easel, paint brush still in hand, a resolute smile on his face.

On hearing the news, Angela and I drove up to his cottage to see if we could do anything to help. We pushed open the front door, went through to the bedroom/studio and over to the easel which was still in place.

Nothing in the room had been touched and, as we rounded the easel to observe his final work, we were surprised and delighted to see what must have been the last thing he ever saw: our complete family group gathered around a broadly-beaming little Chloe – his final source of inspiration.

THE APPLE CORE ENIGMA

It was a quiet Wednesday afternoon in May in the sleepy provincial town of Malingford, a town some 50 miles from Central London and well above the national average in terms of prosperity, property prices, professional people and general wealth. A steady drizzle was falling on the tree-lined drive leading up to the imposing Victorian mansion at the end of exclusive Beechwood Grove. A shadowy figure emerged from behind a large oak tree and discreetly approached the front porch. He knew that the owner, Brendan Williamson, a well-to-do Tory MP, would be in the House of Commons and that his family were enjoying a fortnight's holiday in the Caribbean.

The darkly-clad individual approached the front door, seemed to embrace the main lock, listened to the metallic click and then did the same thing with the back-up locks. He eased the door open and slipped into the entrance hall where he immediately ascertained that the burglar alarm had not been armed. Careless omission! He would, however, almost certainly have been able to deal with the situation had the security device been operative. He was, after all, an expert in security, locks and alarm systems.

Once inside the house, he quickly located Williamson's office. Within a matter of minutes he had found a wall-safe, unimaginatively concealed behind a picture on the wall beside the desk. A short while later, he had cracked the combination of the safe and pulled open the door. He removed three thick wads of used banknotes as well as a drawstring velvet bag containing watches, jewellery, gold coins and a considerable number of small ingots. These he placed in the soft leather briefcase he was carrying, closed and re-locked the safe, stepped back and straightened the picture. Before leaving the room he put his gloved hand in his pocket, took out a simple brass curtain ring and placed it visibly in the centre of the desk. He then exited the house, locked the front door and walked off into the afternoon drizzle.

When Brendan Williamson returned home in the early evening he went through his normal routine: he unlocked the front door, removed his coat, poured himself a large whisky and made for his study to see if there were any missed phone calls. He sat down at his desk and reached for the phone but his attention was drawn to a small yellow ring that he didn't recognise. This gave him an uneasy feeling and his first instinct was to check the contents of his safe. He dialled up the combination and opened the door. He recoiled in shock as he ascertained that the black velvet bag was no longer there. A large number of banknotes had also disappeared.

When the police arrived, he assured them that he had not moved anything in the house. The front door had been locked in the normal way, no windows had been forced and nothing else appeared to have been taken. What really perplexed him was that a small brass ring had been left in the middle of his desk.

Detective Chief Inspector Davidson called forensics in and they carried out a thorough examination of the house, particularly the study and the front door. They found nothing that was likely to be of any assistance; even the curtain ring bore no trace of a fingerprint and they, too, failed to understand its significance except, perhaps, to draw attention to the fact that there had been an intruder in the house. They remained totally baffled.

The following day an insurance agent visited the house and assessed the claim to be somewhere between £190,000 and £200,000.

About an hour's drive from Williamson's house, the sleepy town of Brindleton went about its business as usual. Grant Russell had recently moved there and lived alone in a small block of flats. Apparently he had no family and his parents had been killed in a car crash some years before. Quiet and courteous, this baby-faced writer was in his mid-thirties. He clearly liked to keep himself fit and went running each morning. Apart from that, he spent most of the time in his apartment except at weekends when he took his black Ford Fiesta and drove for about an hour to an isolated retreat he rented to concentrate on his writing, mainly historical fiction he explained to the few people who had got to know him a little.

Russell was sitting in his kitchen drinking coffee and looking through the website of the regional newspaper as he did each morning. He glanced at the sports section, checked on local politics and building projects, read about several cultural events and went on to delve into the general news section. In one article he read about an audacious burglary in Malingford. Russell read it with interest, fascinated by the modus operandi and ingenuity of the thief. He finished up by consulting the week's offerings at the local cinema and poured himself another cup of coffee. Two days later he drove the 30 miles to the secluded cottage he rented through the Internet, located in the heart of some dense woodlands well off the beaten track.

The following Wednesday afternoon, a dark figure made its way across the fields to a sprawling bungalow, home of an eccentric retired army general and his wife who lived up a quiet lane in a small village outside Malingford. The darkly clad figure had observed them for some time and knew their habits well, including the fact that they went out for a constitutional walk every day after lunch and also that they left the door key under a flower pot beside the front door. Nothing could be simpler; he picked the key up and let himself into the house.

In the likely absence of a safe, he turned his attention to a metal cabinet in one corner of the study. The lock was no problem for him and he found what he was looking for. The general was well known locally to be a very keen philatelist and his collection of rare stamps had been conservatively valued at

£250,000. It was now in the hands of his uninvited guest.

He put the albums in the soft leather bag he had brought, placed a ring on the centre of the coffee table and helped himself to a juicy apple from the cut-glass fruit bowl. He nibbled on the apple before leaving the house, locked the door behind him, slid the key under the flower pot and walked back down the garden path. At the gate he took a final bite of the apple and tossed the core deep into the middle of a thick laurel hedge.

By 4 o'clock the thief was back in Malingford and the elderly couple had returned to their house. Mystified by the discovery of the ring on the coffee table, they realised there must have been an intruder and called the police. A quick search revealed what had been taken and forensics set about their routine task. This included the garden and surrounding area, and one of the officers was seen bagging up several items, including a recently discarded apple core.

The General assured the police that neither he nor his wife would have thrown an apple core down in the garden, yet it was the only thing that offered them any help at all. Back in the police laboratories, the technicians set about their work and found a clearly identifiable DNA profile on the core. They consulted the data banks and were very excited when they finally found a match. Records showed that it belonged to a certain Grant Russell who had been tested voluntarily when he had worked as a journalist on a daily newspaper. A female colleague had been sexually assaulted in the newspaper's underground car park and all the male employees had been asked to provide a sample for analysis. He had been totally exonerated but his profile had remained on file.

Early next morning once the DNA had been identified and Russell's current address researched, Inspector Davidson led a team of detectives, both uniformed and plain clothes, to the small town of Brindleton. They surrounded the writer's apartment building, sealed all the exits, prepared to force the door, if necessary, and hammered on the knocker.

The door was opened and Russell recoiled at the sight that greeted him. Half a dozen burly policemen burst into his apartment and immediately surrounded him. DCI Davidson introduced himself and presented his identity card.

"Mr Grant Russell?"

"Yes."

"We would like to ask you some questions, if you don't mind."

"No problem, Inspector. What can I do to help you?"

"Can you tell me where you were yesterday afternoon?"

"Yesterday afternoon? Of course I can. I am a part-time lecturer at the local college and I was giving a tutorial to a group of students."

"And someone will be able to confirm this?"

"Certainly. About 15 people."

The Inspector was somewhat taken aback and tried another approach, "And last Wednesday, also in the afternoon. Can you tell me where you were then, Mr Russell?"

"Yes, I believe so but let me just check my diary. That's right, I was playing golf with three friends. We were playing a foursome all afternoon."

"And your friends can vouch for this?"

"Yes, I'm sure they will. I can give you their details if you like. Could you tell me why you are asking me all these questions, Inspector?"

"Just following up a lead, Mr Russell, and we might need to speak to you again at a later date. I'm sorry to have bothered you."

On leaving the property, the Inspector's feelings were a mixture of puzzlement and embarrassment. He ordered his colleagues back to headquarters, made a number of fruitless phone calls and returned irritably to his own office. He and his assistant, Sergeant Robinson, reviewed everything they knew about the mysterious intruder, especially the question of his DNA, and it didn't really amount to very much.

Normal routine matters took over again at police headquarters and so it continued until, perhaps not surprisingly, the following Wednesday afternoon.

Micky Johnston was a very successful and well known steeplechase jockey. He went away to race meetings several times a week, often sleeping away from home. His wife always travelled with him and acted as his personal assistant. The Johnstons lived several miles outside Malingford in a converted 18th century farmhouse that stood in its own grounds, well away from its nearest neighbours. They had driven off early that morning for another day of busy activity so nobody was likely to see the small saloon car approach the house and park behind it. Their visitor entered a barn at the end of the house and found an old door that gave access to the main building. This he easily unlocked and, once inside, made sure that there was no alarm system.

He knew he had plenty of time to explore the property and started with the trophy cabinet. The centre piece immediately seized his attention; it was a replica of the Gold Cup that Johnston had won the previous year. This soon found its way into his leather bag as did two pairs of gold cuff-links, a diamond bracelet, a vintage Ming vase, a gem-encrusted dagger, and a considerable amount of money, as he went systematically from room to room. He left his tell-tale ring visibly on a polished table in the hall, zipped up his bag and casually strolled back to his waiting car.

After the third 'ring' robbery, the story went national. All the papers carried it and it featured prominently on their websites. In the absence of a suspect, a popular daily carried the headline, 'The Ringman Strikes Again,' and henceforward that was how he became known. Grant Russell followed the case closely, especially the Internet buzz, and was developing a growing admiration for the perpetrator. Because of the apparent DNA match, he was again questioned by DCI Davidson but, once again, had the perfect alibi; he had been helping handicapped children in the local community centre. Furthermore, as all the robberies had been committed on Wednesday afternoons, Russell determined to have a clearly visible public presence on subsequent Wednesdays.

Judge Reginald Willoughby was a busy man. Rich, elegant and charming, he was now in his mid-fifties and, although he was known to have had a number of 'flings' as he liked to call them, he had remained a bachelor, devoting most of his spare time to a deep appreciation of the arts, particularly music and painting. He was an accomplished pianist in his own right and an excellent water colour artist. He lived in a £3,000,000 Georgian house four miles out of Malingford and was currently hearing a high-profile case in town.

As the Ringman approached the house through the woods surrounding it, he was filled with a sense of anticipation. His suspicions were confirmed when he saw a metallic plaque above the main entrance warning the curious that the house was protected by an alarm system. He saw this rather as a challenge and felt certain that he would be able to handle the situation. There were three reasons for his confidence; firstly he believed that, from a distance of ten feet, he could disable the alarm by jamming the signals with radio noise and preventing them from passing from the sensors to the control panel; failing that, he might be able to carry out a 'crash and smash' attack by finding the control panel within a limited time frame and smashing it. If that didn't work, he assumed that the police response time over a distance of four miles would enable him to finish the job without being disturbed.

As he entered the house and no alarm broke the stillness of the afternoon, he assumed the jamming process had been successful. He did a quick tour of the property and saw what he had been hoping to find. Taking pride of place on a wall in the lounge was a magnificent collection of Antique Portrait

Miniatures. The Ringman carefully removed them from the wall, placed them in his bag and, satisfied with his exceptional haul, left his usual signature ring on an occasional table near the front door and went on his way.

The series of break-ins now made second position in the evening TV news bulletins as well as featuring more and more prominently on numerous websites. Russell read them all with interest and was glad he had decided to visit the dentist for a check-up on Wednesday afternoon. This had been followed by a leisurely coffee in a nearby cafe with friends.

DCI Davidson continued to lead the investigation but was barely any further forward in the case. The presence of the brass rings particularly mystified him but he was convinced that they must have some sort of significance. But what could that possibly be?

7h30 Wednesday morning. A Mercedes S600 glided noiselessly out of the underground garage, turned right and headed off into the traffic. At the wheel sat Sir James Pendleton, a rich industrialist and self-made man. His enterprise specialised in pharmaceuticals and boasted over a thousand employees. His departure had just been observed by a dark figure lurking in the shadows on the other side of the street. The Ringman was preparing for his afternoon's work. Opposite him was a large block of luxury apartments and, as he crossed the road, his gaze went instinctively to the 6th floor penthouse. He felt sure that it would have an elaborate security system and he wanted to take a look.

As he stepped out onto the pavement, blondish hair, rimless glasses, well-trimmed moustache, none of the passers-by gave him a second glance. He pulled up the hood of his jacket and approached the entrance to the building. He ran his finger down the list of names until he found the one he wanted. He rang the bell. A voice was heard clearly through the intercom, "Sir James Pendleton's apartment. This is Conchita speaking." The visitor explained that he was from the maintenance department of the security company and that he had come to check Sir James's alarm system. The door clicked, he pushed it open and took the lift to the 6th floor.

He rang the bell. The door opened to reveal a rotund, dark haired woman in her late 50's who smiled and let him in. "Good morning, Conchita," he said returning her smile. "What a beautiful dress. I love the colours." She was flattered and smiled again. Three minutes later, he knew that Conchita was Portuguese, that she was Sir James's cleaner, that she would be leaving at midday and that Sir James himself would not be returning until later that evening. She then showed him the alarm control panel which was concealed in a hallway cupboard. He said that he would be working for about 15 minutes and that she should return to whatever chores she was doing. He pulled on a pair of latex gloves and then set about disabling the alarm, at the same time making sure that it would give the right audio signal in the apartment when the code was re-introduced. He took a quick look at the locks on the main door, allowed himself a contented nod and called to Conchita. She saw him to the door, all the time smiling at the charming maintenance man who had admired her dress.

At 2 o'clock that same day, the "maintenance man" was back again. Without difficulty he entered the apartment and began a systematic search. Now that he knew the alarm was disarmed he felt safe to wander round at his leisure. He saw numerous items of interest but had come for just one reason: Fabergé eggs. In the study stood a large mahogany show case and in the centre of it were two magnificent antique eggs. Sir James must have had complete confidence in his alarm system, so much so that he did not even bother to lock the display cabinet. The Ringman helped himself to the eggs and took a few pieces of ancient silverware for good measure. Before leaving, he placed his ring in the middle of the shelf where the eggs had been.

This time there was a glimmer of hope for Inspector Davidson. The apartment block was equipped with CCTV both outside and in the entrance hall. He examined it closely the following morning but was disappointed to observe that the assailant, no doubt aware of the presence of cameras, had kept his hood up and his head down on entering and leaving the building. Nevertheless a distressed Conchita was able to tell him that the aggressor had blond hair, a small moustache and a pair of lightweight spectacles. That was not very much to go on but, on seeing the CCTV images, the housekeeper confirmed that this was almost certainly the man who had come to service the alarm. Other than that, there was once again nothing to further the inquiry: no DNA and no finger prints.

With the theft of the Fabergé eggs, the story had now become the number one item on the National TV

News and it was a very popular topic of conversation. People were intrigued by the audacity and skill of the mysterious character who had now become known as the 'Phantom Ringman.' DCI Davidson scratched his head and wondered how much longer this could go on.

He had to wait another month for the answer to that. During that time there were four more break-ins, all on Wednesday afternoons, in dwellings ranging from a mobile home to a converted church. The pattern was always the same and each time it was mostly cash that disappeared. Four more doors were re-locked after the event, four more signature rings were left in prominent places. No DNA was found and no fingerprints.

Because of the DNA on the apple core they had found in the hedge, the police continued to have serious doubts about Russell and had tailed him every Wednesday afternoon but could not connect him to the robberies in any way. They even wondered if someone was trying to frame him. In desperation, they obtained a surveillance order from the courts to visit the cottage that he rented for his writing sessions. On the Thursday morning following the latest break-in, the Inspector sent three specialist officers to the cottage to set up a listening device and hidden camera to enable them to monitor the situation from a distance at the weekend when Russell would be in residence. While they were in the cottage they took a number of DNA samples and, when the results subsequently came through, they were bewildered to ascertain that they all matched the original apple core profile. Other than that they found nothing suspicious. The shutters were closed, the mailbox empty and there was no sign of any activity.

Early on Saturday morning, Davidson took 15 officers back into the area, parked in the woods several hundred metres from the cottage and began to deploy his men. The shutters were now open, indicating that Russell had probably been there since the previous evening. They moved stealthily through the trees and surrounded the cottage. Sergeant Robinson and two men carefully reconnoitered the building before returning to Davidson with the news that the writer was, indeed, inside and that he appeared to be working on a script. They all returned to their posts, maintained a hidden presence and were told that they would be there for the rest of the day.

Dusk was starting to fall and Davidson thought he would wait another half hour. In the growing obscurity two dim headlights could be seen coming along the grassy path leading to the house. As they got closer, he could see that it was a small saloon, not unlike the one driven by Russell himself. He could just make out the silhouette of the driver who continued past his observation point and parked around the back of the house, out of sight. Within minutes the curtains had been closed and more lights put on inside.

Inspector Davidson and Sergeant Robinson settled down and waited for events to unfold. They were not to be disappointed. The control screen indicated that the two men were seated at the table. Russell could clearly be seen facing the camera; the other man was directly opposite him and presented only a back view. They listened intently, hoping to find the answers to two key questions: how to explain the presence of Russell's DNA on the apple core and the significance of the brass rings.

Russell was the first to speak: "You know, of course, we won't be able to keep any of this stuff, don't you?"

"No, I suppose we won't."

"But don't worry about it. I've found someone who will take the whole lot from us and pay well for it. Big bucks! We're only going to be interested in cash. But let's face it; we're going to have loads of that. Another month and we'll be living in luxury."

"But how will we be able to carry all that money?"

"Good God, man. Don't even think about it. I've opened an offshore account and it can all be transferred directly," explained Russell. "No problem there."

"Oh, that's great. It's amazing when you think of it, you know. All I can do is open locks and things like that and you do everything else, all the thinking," said his mysterious companion.

"That's what you call team work. We've each had a part to play."

"Yes, but you've had to do so much more: research, planning, picking out the rich guys. Even the disguise was your idea," said the visitor admiringly.

"That's true, but I couldn't have opened even one of those locks. Who knows? Perhaps the Ringman will strike again somewhere else when we get there."

"The Ringman," repeated the other and they had a good laugh at the epithet the press had chosen for him. "I reckon that's something that had them all guessing."

Davidson had heard enough. He silently moved up to the window and was able to see in through a chink in the curtains. He was opposite the camera and from where he stood he could clearly see the recent arrival face on. He could hardly believe his eyes, especially when Russell then stood up and walked round the table. He looked from one face to the other and then back to the first.

In a flash he had solved the case. Identical twins! Identical DNA! One apple core!

Two officers were told to bring up a battering ram and within seconds a dozen policemen had invested the cottage.

Apart from the table and chairs, the only item of furniture in the kitchen was a large wooden crockery cabinet which had been moved to one side by the two men, revealing a hidden door giving direct access to a wall cupboard. Davidson opened the door, looked inside and picked up a soft leather bag. He unzipped it and withdrew an interesting collection of items including numerous wads of money, watches, jewellery, Fabergé eggs, miniatures and other precious objects – a veritable treasure trove. In a box on the floor he found a blond wig, a pair of rimless glasses, a neatly-trimmed false moustache, the remains of a large packet of latex gloves and a small box of curtain rings. All that in addition to a book on the installation and maintenance of various alarm systems.

A further search produced two passports and two one-way business class tickets to Australia, dated one month hence. Davidson opened the first passport and, recognising the face, saw that it was in the name of Grant Russell. The mystery of the rings was elucidated when he opened the second passport and turned to the identity page. He saw a familiar face staring unsmilingly back at him but, when he looked at the name beside it, he recoiled in surprise, allowing himself a wry smile as he read what was obviously a pseudonym, "Michael John Ringer."

The irony was lost on no one.

THE OFFICIAL GUIDE

Henry Braithwaite felt very proud as he turned up for the first day in his new job. He was going to work as a guide in a most prestigious stately home and that morning he had gargled long and hard to clarify his vocals. He thrust his chest out in delight as he walked into the Administrative Offices and was given his Official Guide's hat; he particularly appreciated the word "OFFICIAL" emblazoned in gold lettering just above the peak. He invited his group of about 20 visitors to form a semi-circle around him, all the better to hear his commentary and his answers to their questions.

Henry began the tour by explaining something of the history of the house. "The building itself dates from the very beginning of its creation. You'd be surprised just how old it really is. In fact it pre-dates all other houses built after it and could well be the oldest building in the whole area. It was constructed using only local materials, all of which were sourced within the British Isles. The wood was taken exclusively from mature trees which were felled using nothing but traditional methods. The stonework was quarried from below ground level and worked by stonemasons into the required shapes. The angle of the roof is particularly noteworthy as it slopes right down to the top of the outer walls. The current owner has his apartments in a private section of the house, also built with all the aforementioned materials."

Some of the visitors nodded in appreciation while others seemed a little bemused by what they had just heard. When Henry asked if there were any questions so far, one timid, little old lady, her hair neatly arranged in a greying bun, asked who the current owner actually was. "Ah, that's very interesting indeed," answered Henry. "He is very well known in these parts. He comes from a prestigious family, of course, and can easily be recognised by his physical similarity to a number of his ancestors. His mother was married to his father after betrothal and he was born with the proverbial silver spoon in his mouth."

He paused to give his guests time to absorb what they had just been told. They looked speculatively at each other until a rather loudly-dressed, brash individual inquired, "Just how big is this place anyway? For example, how many rooms are there?"

"Now there's something that will absolutely amaze you," enjoined Henry. "There are far more rooms than you would ever imagine. They're all along the sides of the house with windows on two sides in the corner ones and they open off from the long, carpeted corridors. All the doors open inwards and the windows are on the opposite side of the room. The rooms on the second floor are smaller because some of the ground floor ones are more spacious, for example the ballroom and the dining hall. In fact the largest room is at least ten times the size of the smaller ones. Then you must not forget the kitchens, store-rooms and cellars that are in the basement. Indeed, this is by far the biggest house in this beautiful park which is so exclusive that it has no other buildings in it."

As they rounded the corner at the end of a corridor, they came upon a very large double window. Henry thought he would point out some of the wonders of the gardens from there. "As you might observe, the park contains a small lake, numerous paths, multiple trees, bushes, shrubs and flowers. There is also a very large expanse of grass to be seen. We employ more than just a single gardener and they have the use of some very modern equipment. The result of all that, as you can see, is quite spectacular."

Someone from the back of the group raised a tentative hand. "Who was the architect?"

"Good question," was the official guide's response. "Not surprisingly, he was extremely well known. You've all heard of Christopher Wren, Inigo Jones and people like that. Well, this man was right up there with the best of them, a real innovator, a revolutionary. He did his best work towards the end of his career and that explains why this place is so much in advance of its time."

There was a momentary hiatus while Henry paused for breath. Another visitor took advantage of this to ask how many guests could be accommodated at the same time. "Well, let's just say that there are enough bedrooms to give one to every guest. Obviously more people could stay if they shared rooms or came to visit at another time."

A balding individual with a strange accent and an over-sized smirk on his face thought he would catch Henry out with his question: "What about ghosts then? All big, old, country houses are supposed to have one, aren't they? What about this place? Do you have any here?"

Henry thought for a moment before replying, "Until you can prove that there isn't one, there's always a chance that there might be. You're correct in thinking that many country houses are believed to have a resident ghost and this house could well fall into that category. If he suddenly appears now, you'll be able to see him for yourselves and you'll be left in no doubt on this particular matter."

And so the tour continued; rooms were visited, commentary was given, questions were asked, answers were expounded and before long it was time to conclude. Henry thanked his guests for their visit and noticed how preoccupied they all seemed to be. As he looked around from face to face, he saw signs of astonishment and had the distinct impression that some of them would like to come back again to learn more. This made him feel very proud of all the fascinating information he had been able to deliver to them during the tour.

They were heading slowly towards the exit when Henry delivered his final gem. "Just one more thing, ladies and gentlemen. There is a cafeteria next to the main entrance where you can purchase something to eat and drink on the way out. That is, of course, for those of you who might be hungry or thirsty."

He stood near the door of the room as they were leaving, holding his hand out optimistically as they passed him by. One or two shook it weakly, several refused to even make eye contact with him and most just walked past him with a quizzical look on their faces. Another was scratching his head in a gesture of incomprehension, whilst two more stared straight ahead, wearing an expression of absolute incredulity.

Things moved quickly. In the space of a single tour, Henry had forged a reputation for himself, a reputation that now preceded him as he strode back into the Administrative Offices. Feeling very satisfied with himself after a good morning's work, he hung his Official Guide's hat back upon a peg and smiled broadly at the Director who met his gaze and slowly shook his head before saying, "Mr Braithwaite. Please go out that door and look for a small wooden building to get your money. You won't find anything there as it hasn't actually been built yet. But just use your imagination a little and enjoy spending the money."

As Henry went through the door, smiling to himself, the Director called after him, "Oh, and by the way, Mr Braithwaite, don't forget NOT to come back again."

THE LITTLE BLACK DOG

A cold December evening in 1962. A steady drizzle had been falling for hours. It was Friday night and the thought of another miserable weekend already began to depress Peter Baxter.

It was just after 20h15 when he came out of the bar and turned into Regent Street. He had left the office as usual at 18h00 but had called in at the "Cat and Fiddle" for a drink because he needed time to think. Now, after two hours of lonely meditation, he felt just as dejected.

He walked past a famous couturier's and caught a glimpse of himself in a mirror at the back of the window display. A skinny, balding clerk in his late 30's, huddled in a blue serge raincoat and woollen muffler, he looked so incongruous among the mannequins and colourful dresses. It was not unusual for him to look and feel out of place wherever he went but at this precise moment he was not concerned about his physical appearance; he had another problem and, although he'd had it for only a few hours, it eclipsed all his normal preoccupations.

That afternoon the chief clerk had not given him his wage packet as he normally did. Instead, he had told him that Mr Pringle wanted to see him in his office. Mr Pringle was Managing Director, not only because he knew the right people and said the right things, but because he had the ruthless streak necessary to be successful. Baxter could have accepted all this but he always had the impression that Mr Pringle despised his junior employees. As he walked towards the Tube Station he relived for the umpteenth time their brief, one-sided conversation.

"You wanted to see me, Mr Pringle?"

"Yes, Baxter. Sit down, will you?"

From Pringle's reply he knew that some important matter was about to be broached. A problem with his work? A move to another department? Perhaps even a promotion? Who could tell? Normally he would have been left to stand and shift uncomfortably from one leg to the other. He felt hardly more at ease now as he sat under the Managing Director's piercing gaze.

"I'm afraid I have some bad news for you and I prefer to come straight to the point. Because of unfortunate and unforeseeable circumstances we are obliged to cut down on personnel in all our offices. Since you have not been with us as long as the other clerks I'm afraid you will be made redundant as from December 23rd when we begin our Christmas break. That means one week from today. We appreciate your work and will be giving you a little bonus when you leave us; you'll be receiving an additional fortnight's salary. I'm sorry."

Mr Pringle picked up his pen and continued writing to show Baxter that the interview was at an end.

"I see," said Baxter, "Thank you," and he rose to return to his desk in the main office.

He now recalled Pringle's supercilious face in the cold December night and wondered why he had said 'thank you' as if the man were doing him a favour. 'Unfortunate and unforeseeable circumstances . . . . little bonus'. He was sure the Managing Director wasn't unduly worried about the unfortunate circumstances. Pringle would still get his grossly exaggerated annual bonus, and two weeks' pay wasn't going to make that much difference to Baxter. He thrust his hands deep in his coat pockets and slouched along towards Piccadilly Circus.

Nothing less than a screech of brakes and the sound of shattering glass could have penetrated the mantle of wretchedness that now enveloped Peter Baxter. A high-powered sports car turning into Regent Street had tried to beat the changing lights, skidded on the slippery surface, gone out of control and crashed through the window of a travel agency; only the rear end of the car protruded onto the pavement. By the time Baxter came abreast of what remained of the shop-front, a small crowd had already gathered. Perhaps it was the thought of seeing someone else's misfortune that drew him irresistibly towards the confused scene. Most of the people were trying to get a better view of the driver who was unconscious and bleeding profusely from the head. As Baxter threaded his way among them, his eye fell on a large coloured poster that filled the only part of the window left intact.

With a background of snowy peaks and an azure sky such as Baxter had never seen, an attractive girl invited passers-by, invited him, to enjoy the 'Holiday of a Lifetime - Winter Sports in Sunny Switzerland'. He glanced at the driver of the car who was starting to groan weakly but the girl's eyes seemed to follow him and he looked back at the poster. He could see little wooden chalets dotted all over the mountainside, majestic evergreens capped with snow and sun-tanned skiers gliding gracefully down the slopes. But above all he couldn't take his eyes off the beautiful girl with the seductive smile. It seemed to him like another world, perhaps one that, with the firm's 'little bonus' he might even be able to penetrate. Baxter had never been in love, had never even had a girlfriend; the only romance he had ever known had been with girls on chocolate boxes or in toothpaste advertisements. Perhaps this was the start of a new affair.

Twenty minutes later the ambulance had left the scene and most of the people had dispersed. Baxter realised that the "Come on, sir, move along please" was directed at him. He was still deep in thought as he wandered aimlessly up the nearest side street and into another bar. He slumped down onto a stool and ordered a whisky. This was followed by another, despite the fact that he rarely drank anything except for the occasional glass of beer. The effect of the drink helped him to forget that in one week he would be out of work and, the less he thought of this, the more he thought about the girl in the poster. It was not until around 11 o'clock that he stepped out into the chill night air and, as he rounded the bend into Piccadilly Circus, he was dazzled by a million neon lights, flashing, spinning, blinding. He felt as if he were reeling madly, all alone on a crazy carousel. Three faces emerged from the blur of colour: a pompous manager, an injured motorist and a beautiful foreigner.

As the train came to a halt at Balham Station, Baxter's subconscious, which had been counting the stops, pushed him out the door and into the relentless drizzle of suburban London. Fifteen minutes later he was opening the front door of the old three-storey house in which he rented a bedsit. He had been there since he first came to London four years earlier. He had only intended to stay for a few weeks while he looked for something better but the price had been right and he hadn't really felt the need to change. He had never known his father and, when his mother died, he had left Wiltshire for the big city, hoping to make a fresh start there and find a way of brightening up his cheerless existence. He often regretted the move but always tried to convince himself that things must surely change for the better. And now he was just as lonely and without a job.

The nervous strain of the afternoon together with an abnormal quantity of alcohol soon plunged him into a deep sleep; so deep that it could not last. He awoke with a parched throat and turned on the light. Twenty past one a.m. He groped his way to the communal bathroom and drank several glasses of water. He went back to bed and lay there trying to doze off but his mind began to wander over the events of the previous day. He put Pringle out of his mind and found himself thinking about the Swiss Alps again. What was it that appealed to him so much? The country? The thought of escaping? The girl? Or just the idea of doing something different? The nearest he had ever come to going abroad was two days on the Isle of Wight and a cancelled day trip to Boulogne. Suddenly he was filled with an uncontrollable sense of adventure. He would give Pringle and the rest of them something to think about. This day was going to mark the beginning of a new life – a new Baxter. Losing his job might just turn out to be a blessing in disguise. Long live redundancy!

It often happens that the plans one makes in the reassuring comfort of one's bed seem absurd in the light of a new day. Such was not the case for Peter Baxter. Saturday, 17th of December, was to be a day of action. The decision had been made; there now remained the simple formality of visiting the travel agency, making his reservation and then using the following week's 'little bonus' to finance his adventure. This could be the start of a new life!

It was only as he finished shaving that he realised he was singing. He tried to recall the first verse of a recent pop song, couldn't remember the words and resorted to 'Oh, What a Beautiful Morning!' He smiled to himself in the mirror, carefully parted his thinning hair, selected a maroon tie to go with a clean white shirt and gave his shoes a quick polish.

The agency closed at 1 o'clock but he had plenty of time to get there as he had got up earlier than usual. He felt energetic and decided to go the long way to the station. This meant walking round the factory, past the primary school and along the railway embankment. It was a walk he always enjoyed, especially when it was quiet and the factory and school were closed. He walked with a spring in his step, had a cheery word for the mailman and ruffled the hair of a small boy who ran into him while chasing his football. He thought dispassionately about Mr Pringle. He no longer felt any resentment; after all, the man had his job to do like everyone else.

He particularly thought about Switzerland. He wondered where he would be in a fortnight, what language the people around him would be speaking, what new dishes he would be savouring. He grinned at the thought that the girl in the poster was probably a photographic model who had never even been to Switzerland. Still, the fact remained that she had given him the inspiration and he now felt happy.

He spared a thought for the injured driver and felt a little guilty that he had not been able to offer any help. But then, what could he have done anyway? He soon forgot the motorist and whistled to himself as he walked along by the railway embankment.

He had reached the point where he had to cross the double track. The road, which had been rising for some time, now turned abruptly to the right and went over the lines before veering again to follow the same general direction on the other side of the tracks. The rails were no longer visible on his left as the bridge he had just crossed also marked the beginning of a short tunnel. As he neared the end of the tunnel the road dropped down again to the level of the railway.

On the other side of the track a toddler shrieked with joy as he rode on his father's shoulders and reached for the sky. Baxter turned instinctively to look across at them. In an instant his amusement changed to horror. In his peripheral vision he had noticed a little black terrier lying beside the railway line near the exit of the tunnel. Oblivious to the potential danger it faced, it showed no sign of moving away. He picked up a stone and threw it in the direction of the dog. His aim was poor and the creature didn't move.

Terror welled up inside him as he knew a train might emerge from the tunnel at any moment. He had to do something. He couldn't just let the dog stay there and get crushed. He hated to see suffering in animals; they weren't like speeding sports car drivers. His heart pounded as the sense of urgency increased.

There was a narrow footpath leading down to the track. He scrambled over the fence and down the embankment. He jumped over some brambles and leapt towards the dog that still hadn't moved.

At that precise moment a suburban train thundered out of the tunnel and continued inexorably in a southerly direction. It was soon lost over the distant horizon and the stillness of the morning was broken only by the gentle rustling of the nearby trees.

Any contact, albeit a glancing blow, with a hundred tons of steel travelling at 80 miles an hour can have only one consequence.

Peter Baxter was killed outright.

"I'm sorry to drag you in here at such short notice, Mr Pringle," said DCI Handley, "especially on a Saturday, but I'm sure you understand."

Pringle was sorry, too, because he was just about to leave for the country when the phone had rung.

Still, it built up his prestige a little, he was always happy to represent the firm and he managed a weak smile.

"From papers found on the body," continued the Inspector, "it seems his name was Peter Baxter. His landlady hardly knew him but assured me that he had no relatives. She said he didn't communicate much and always struck her as being particularly taciturn. She suggested I contact you as apparently he worked for your firm."

"Yes, that's right," said Pringle. "He was one of our clerks. But only yesterday we had to give him his notice. Question of cutting down on staff, you know."

"I see," said the Inspector. "That rather confirms what we already suspected. Would you mind coming with me? I'm afraid I must ask you to identify the body."

Pringle was surprised at how little it had been mutilated. What intrigued him most was that he had never seen Baxter looking so relaxed. There was even the suggestion of a smile on his face.

They returned to the Inspector's office and spoke briefly about personality, redundancy, depression and suicide. The Inspector seemed to be satisfied with his conclusions, picked up the telephone and gave an order liberating the officers who had remained on duty by the railway embankment.

"Just as well, if you ask me," said the sergeant in charge, as they climbed back up the narrow path leading to the road. "Waste of time, that was. The only thing we've come up with after nearly three hours is a child's cuddly toy − a little black dog!"

THE NEW BOY

Young Jonny Martin was 12 years old. His father was a French diplomat, his mother English and an executive secretary. They had arrived in England only two days earlier and this was to be the first day in his new secondary school, always an exciting, if somewhat daunting, day in the life of a young boy.

Jonny's father was currently travelling and, by an unfortunate coincidence, his mother had to attend a crucial board meeting that same Monday morning. She had, therefore, arranged with a local taxi firm for her son to be picked up and taken to school and also to be brought home again at the end of the day. Before she left for her appointment, she rang the taxi company again to make sure that they would be on time and that everything was in order. It was.

His mother had to leave at 7h30 but she left Jonny in the care of their live-in house-maid, Nadine, whom he had known all his life. His transport duly arrived at 8 o'clock and a pleasant, middle-aged man identified himself and escorted Jonny to the waiting vehicle. He said the trip would take about 15 minutes and joined in with the main flow of traffic.

He dropped Jonny at the school gates and assured him that he would be there at 4 o'clock to take him back home. Jonny stood there for a moment, looking at the impressive complex of buildings before him. Despite his young age, he was quite self-assured and he walked confidently through the huge doors of the main building into the bustling throng of excited students. After a few minutes, they were all ushered into the school's gymnasium to be assigned to their various class groups. He was conscious of several other languages being spoken but had been used to that all his life.

He was called over by one of the teachers carrying a clip board with a sheaf of papers attached to it bearing class lists and other information.

"Hello. What's your name then?"

"Jonny Martin, sir."

"Right. Let's see where you have to go."

But, try as he might, he couldn't find Jonny's name anywhere. He double checked and still found nothing. Having established that, considering his age, he should be in class 7, the first year of secondary school, the teacher told him to go to a desk with a large number 7 hanging above it and speak to Miss Downing, the year head in charge of the four 7th grade classes. She smiled at him to reassure him but she, too, failed to find his name anywhere. In the end she decided to inscribe him provisionally in one of the groups and told him to go to room 107.

There he was greeted by the class master, Mr Taylor, an enthusiastic young man who was to be their English teacher. He explained to the class that they would see four other teachers during the day in addition to himself. He gave them details of their timetable, told them about lunch arrangements, PE equipment, homework requirements and all the other practical things they needed to know. As all the pupils were new to the school, he then asked each of his charges to say a few words by way of introduction. Jonny thought they sounded like an interesting bunch and looked forward to getting to know them better. Towards the end of the morning when all the formalities and administrative details had been satisfactorily dealt with, Mr Taylor told Jonny to go to room 214 and ask to see the Principal's secretary in an attempt to sort out the question of his registration.

Once again there was no trace of his name anywhere and in the end he was simply added to Mr Taylor's class list, at least until the problem could be sorted out.

Lunch time. The whole of class 7 were told to be in the dining hall at 12h30. Jonny sat at a table with five others from his class and they started to exchange personal details. His classmates were impressed to hear of all the countries he had visited and lived in as a result of his father's profession. Some of them had never even been abroad. He was establishing himself as the dominant character in their little group and rather enjoyed the attention; it made him feel good.

After lunch the class were told they would meet the teachers of Maths, PE, French and Geography during the course of the afternoon; they would explain the aims and expectations of their particular subjects.

Maths was first and Miss Russell thought she would try a little mental arithmetic to get some idea of the class's basic knowledge. She started with some simple multiplications and was pleased to see so many hands going up to volunteer an answer. As the questions became more challenging, the raised hands became fewer and fewer until there were only two or three willing to risk their self-esteem. Jonny was one of them. Miss Russell was pleased with what she had witnessed and showed them the text book they would be using and the equipment they would need.

Next came the PE master, Harry Jenson. His head was shaven, his muscles bristled and he was just a little brash. The class could clearly see it would not be wise to upset this man.

The French teacher, Monsieur Dubois, said a few words in French as if to impress the class, asked them if anyone could speak the language and, when Jonny raised a finger in response, he was invited to try his hand. He, of course, spoke French at home and decided to relate, at some speed, a description of his favourite holiday destination. Monsieur Dubois was agape; he didn't quite know how to react and felt his own confidence slowly ebbing away.

The last visitor of the day was Mrs. Henderson, the Geography specialist. She, in turn, outlined her plans for the year and, in order to stimulate their interest in travelling and their knowledge of different places, she initiated a discussion on the different places the members of the class had visited. Though many of them could claim to have visited a foreign destination, Jonny's list, by contrast, sounded more like the index to a world atlas.

In fact he had impressed the people he encountered all day, both teachers and students, and had already earned something of a reputation for himself, not least because of his missing registration documents.

At the end of the day, he walked along to the school entrance, located the parked taxi, greeted the driver and climbed inside. Fifteen minutes later the car pulled up outside his house and Nadine let him in and gave him something to eat and drink. His mother arrived home at ten past five, keen to know how his first day at school had gone.

"Well, Jonny, did you have a good time in school?"

"Yes, it was fine but there was something a bit funny about it."

"And what was that?"

"Well, they didn't have my name on any of their lists. Nobody seemed to know anything about me."

"That's strange," replied his mother. "We arranged all that at least four weeks ago. There shouldn't have been any problems. Anyway, did you enjoy it?"

"Yes, I guess I did, really."

"Good," said his mother with finality. "And, in any case, I'll be able to take you along myself tomorrow. I'll go in and speak to them about it, to see what happened."

Next morning, at ten to eight, Mme Martin reversed her BMW out of the garage and joined the traffic on the main road. She had barely gone 200 metres when Jonny exclaimed:

"Wait a minute, Mum. Stop the car. We're going the wrong way."

Surprised by his insistence, she pulled over at the first opportunity to hear him out. Jonny was adamant that the taxi driver had gone in the opposite direction on leaving the house. She was still unfamiliar with the neighbourhood and Jonny seemed so convinced that she assumed the driver must have known a short cut or a less crowded road. Jonny promised her he would remember exactly how to get to the school again.

"It's very easy really," he said. "Go past the house again, carry on to the second traffic lights, turn left and continue on for about four kilometres. You can see the school on the right hand side of the road, just after a big church."

And that is exactly what she did. She followed his instructions to the letter, saw the imposing campus on the other side of the road and pulled into a lay-by. She looked quizzically across at the main gates and exclaimed, "But that's not your school! Look at the name above the entrance. 'International Secondary School'. You're going to the French Lycée!"

She sighed, but there was the clear suggestion of a wry smile on her face. "I think I know what happened yesterday; the taxi company must have got the names confused!"

HEIST

The birth of our little boy, Tommy, had been a difficult one for my wife, Cristina. At first there were even fears for his survival but after a few weeks he had rallied and was now a thriving 14 month old toddler. In order to celebrate the family stability we now enjoyed, we decided to take a 10-day cruise out of Miami, sailing round the Eastern Caribbean. Cristina's parents generously paid for a cabin upgrade and offered us a mini-suite with balcony.

We had booked in with the Sensational Cruise Line and were due to sail on the 'Ultimate Sensation', calling in at a selection of Caribbean islands. This was our first such trip and, as we stepped out of the taxi at the cruise ship terminal, we were staggered to see the 14-deck behemoth towering above us. Immigration formalities completed, we wheeled Tommy along the quayside, up the loading ramp onto a lower deck, into an elevator and up to deck 10 where we were informed we would find our stateroom.

We could not have wished for more comfortable accommodation: king-sized bed, luxurious bathroom, sitting area with small table and leather armchairs, folding cot for Tommy, writing desk and fitted wardrobes, all decorated in a highly-polished veneer finish. A sliding door gave on to the generously dimensioned private balcony. We could see why the 'Ultimate Sensation' was recognized as the company's flagship.

Once we were comfortably installed in our stateroom and as there were still several hours before sailing time, we set off to explore the rest of the ship. Though we had read all about the amenities in a brochure, it was truly amazing to see everything that was on offer. Among other facilities, we discovered nine restaurants, various other eateries, four swimming pools, a 1250-seater theatre, a health spa, a nursery, a casino and a sports deck. In addition, there was a very large dining area and that is where we headed at 18h30.

All guests were assigned to a designated table and we found ourselves with six other people plus, of course, little Tommy for whom a high chair had been squeezed in between our places.

Firstly there were the Bakers, Peter and his wife, Margaret; he was a retired Maths teacher, she had been a social worker. They were accompanied by their daughter, Melanie, probably in her early 30's, who was very quiet and worked for an insurance company.

Next came Jeremy and Amanda Ford; he had worked in the theatre in various capacities and had also done a spell as a travelling salesman; she had trained as a hairdresser but had spent a number of years assisting her husband with his work. They had no children and, as they both seemed to be the wrong side of 40, that was likely to remain the case.

Finally there was Robert Crowther, perhaps 35, who preferred to be known by his family name if, indeed, he was obliged to engage in conversation at all; he remained completely noncommittal about his profession and simply muttered something about being in business.

We sailed at 8pm on day one, knowing that the whole of the following day would be spent at sea. At dinner, with the notable exception of Crowther, everyone was really animated, exchanging personal information and eagerly anticipating all the good things to come. He spent most of his time picking at his food and staring at his plate or into the middle distance. He showed no reaction at all to Tommy's latest antics and didn't even look at Melanie who must have been about the same age and was certainly not unattractive. One had to wonder why he had come on a cruise at all and what must have been going through his mind.

Our cruise was to include shore visits to the islands of Grand Turk, Puerto Rico, St Thomas, St Kitts and St Maarten, in that order. Generally speaking, we docked around breakfast time each day and sailed in the early evening, thus allowing time for shore excursions, shopping or simply to relax on the local beaches. The other days would be spent at sea, enjoying the multifarious attractions the ship had to offer us.

Both the Bakers' and the Fords' staterooms were on the same deck as ours and we seemed to bump into them quite a lot. Both couples obviously liked Tommy, and Amanda Ford offered to walk him round the ship in his buggy whenever we wanted her to. It was a generous offer and, although there was something just a little unfathomable about her, Tommy will go to virtually anyone so we said we would gladly take her up on it.

At dinner on day two, after a day at sea exploring the 'Ultimate Sensation', we compared notes and exchanged ideas for the upcoming week. We had checked out the nursery and visited the entertainment centre. The Bakers had spent time enjoying the ozone up on top, walking on the promenade deck and admiring the ultra-modern theatre. Melanie had made a visit to the spa, done a little shopping and got friendly with a group of young people from Europe. The Fords had favoured the pool and sangria bar. What Crowther had done was anyone's guess.

Next morning we docked at Grand Turk where we were to spend most of the day. Fortunately the quayside is right next to the town and beaches so we could just walk off the ship with no need for the tenders to take us ashore. As we and another 2,500 passengers disembarked, we glanced up at the 'Ultimate' and saw what looked more like an enormous apartment block soaring up into the sky. We settled for the beach. I sat in the shade of a friendly palm tree while Tommy splashed around happily at the water's edge and Cristina went searching for a few souvenirs.

By 3h30 we were all back on board. Soon after there was a long blast on the ship's horn and we were under way. Rumour quickly started to spread that there had been an important robbery in a major jeweller's on the island while we were there. At first it was difficult to know what to believe but by dinner time it was generally understood that a large number of diamonds had mysteriously disappeared and the authorities could offer no explanation. Initial reports spoke of several million dollars' worth.

Our next port of call was San Juan, Puerto Rico. We realised this would not be the ideal stopover for little Tommy but, nevertheless, decided to go ashore and take a bus tour of the city. After a while he did, indeed, become irritable and only really settled when we returned to the ship and took him along to the kiddies' pool. That evening he cheered up even more; Amanda had noticed that Tommy was teething and had bought him a multi-coloured teething ring and a little blue teddy bear. He just loved them both and, with a happy chuckle, he put the ring straight in his mouth and started chewing on it. Within a few hours the little bear had become his favourite toy and he insisted on taking it everywhere he went.

Now that we had reached the Eastern Caribbean, we were going to island-hop, visiting a different island on three consecutive days. The main onshore attractions on all of them were duty-free shopping and beautiful beaches. The first one was Saint Thomas, U.S. Virgin Islands, and we docked there early on day five at Charlotte Amalie, a bustling cruise ship port. It was Cristina's birthday and I proposed looking for some ear-rings and a bracelet to go with a necklace she particularly liked. It did not take long to convince her. There was a plethora of jewellers but we found one that had exactly what we were looking for. After lunch we went to a beautiful white sandy beach and, once again, Tommy had a great time. Before returning to the 'Ultimate', we sat on a shady terrace, sipping a banana daiquiri, a local speciality. Tommy made light work of a rather large ice cream. Once back in our stateroom, all 3 of us fell asleep and woke up just in time for dinner.

A real buzz of excitement greeted us as we entered the dining hall. Clearly some major incident had taken place. Before we could even sit down, Peter Baker greeted us with, "Have you heard the latest? It's unbelievable. It's happened again."

"What?" I replied. "What are you talking about?"

"There's been another heist, a robbery."

"And where do you think this time?" enjoined his wife.

"I don't know. Tell me."

"Right here, under our noses again. On St Thomas. Same kind of thing, too."

Apparently we had missed all the excitement. As soon as the news broke, nobody had spoken about anything else. A similar robbery had taken place in one of the biggest jewellers' on St Thomas. The scenario was similar: there had been no violence and a large selection of diamonds, worth a great deal of money, had mysteriously disappeared.

"I don't see how that can possibly happen," said Jeremy Ford. "With CCTV cameras, armed guards and all the rest of it."

"Well, it has happened," his wife added. "At least, that's what everyone is saying. It's the coincidence of it all that I find hard to believe."

And so we continued to discuss the situation throughout the meal, without being any the wiser. Peter and Margaret Baker displayed a mixture of shock, horror and indignation, as if they felt the whole thing personally. Melanie was excited and incredulous at the same time. Jeremy was intrigued and admitted that he had a certain admiration for someone who could get away with it. Amanda didn't really know what to think. Finally it was Peter who looked across the table in the direction of our taciturn companion, "And you, Mr Crowther. What did you do today? Did you go ashore?"

A slight nod.

"What do you think about this whole robbery thing then?"

No reply.

Peter gave up in despair. Crowther remained uncommunicative, preoccupied, introverted, and retired into his own personal world of silence.

A little later, while we were still at table an announcement came over the tannoy system:

THIS IS THE CAPTAIN SPEAKING. PLEASE LISTEN CAREFULLY TO THE FOLLOWING ANNOUNCEMENT. AS YOU ARE NO DOUBT AWARE, TWO VERY SERIOUS ROBBERIES HAVE TAKEN PLACE IN TWO OF THE PORTS WE HAVE VISITED RECENTLY. WITHOUT WISHING TO ALARM ANYONE, I WOULD URGE YOU TO REMEMBER TO USE THE

SAFES LOCATED IN ALL STATEROOMS TO SECURE ALL VALUABLES AND NOT TO LEAVE ANY ITEMS OF VALUE ON ANY OPEN SURFACES. PLEASE UNDERSTAND THAT THIS IS PURELY A PRECAUTIONARY MEASURE AND THAT THERE IS NO REASON TO BE CONCERNED. THANK YOU FOR YOUR ATTENTION. I HOPE YOU WILL ENJOY THE REST OF YOUR CRUISE.

The mood became a little more sombre after the meal as the guests walked discreetly back to their staterooms; they conversed in hushed tones, glanced around nervously and made sure that their doors were securely locked.

Our day at Saint Kitts proved to be uneventful and, it must be admitted, almost something of an anti-climax. Nothing happened. Perhaps the two heists had been a coincidence after all. We had decided to remain on board and just relax. The Fords, too, said they were not going ashore, at least not until after lunch. They offered to look after Tommy for a couple of hours and we gladly accepted, taking advantage of the time to enjoy a relaxing massage and several other pleasures of the spa.

Day seven. St Maarten. Our final visit. A small island that is nonetheless shared between Holland and France, renowned for its timeshares, fabulous beaches and duty-free shopping. We had a full day there and lined up with a multitude of enthusiastic cruisers to go ashore on the tender. We were joining the passengers from several other ships and, from the dock area, followed the heaving mass of humanity into the one Main Street in Philipsburg, the capital. Every shop was a centre of frenetic activity and we decided it was just too much for us. We headed off to the nearest beach, enjoyed lunch on a nearby terrace and took an early tender back to the 'Ultimate'.

From mid-afternoon onwards a steady flow of shoppers filed back to the ship and, with them, the startling breaking news. It had happened again! This time the feeling was more of disbelief. Accounts varied but they all had several things in common: another inexplicable disappearance of diamonds, racing police cars, summary bag searches; in a word, 'chaos'.

By the time we settled down for our evening meal, a number of things had been confirmed: there had, indeed, been another robbery; it was similar to the others, it appeared to be the biggest yet and, perhaps most significantly, only two cruise ships had visited all three ports on the days in question. Ours, of course, was one of them. Inevitably that meant that a certain suspicion had fallen on the 'Ultimate Sensation' and we all started to look at each other interrogatively in what was certainly a more restrained atmosphere. As I looked round the table, the wildest thoughts took control of my imagination. Could the Bakers just be making sure of enjoying a prosperous retirement? Was Melanie's timidity a way of covering up a more aggressive personality? Were the Fords bored with their existence and what did they really do anyway? And where would you even begin with Crowther?

Obviously one topic of conversation dominated all others that evening. Surprisingly, it was Melanie who first broached the subject. "Do you realise?" she said. "It could be someone on this very ship. Someone in this dining room right now!"

"I think there's a very realistic chance of that," replied Jeremy. "Whoever it was must be having dinner somewhere or other.

"I don't reckon they're going to catch him anyway," added Margaret.

At that precise moment I happened to be looking at Crowther. Was there just the suggestion of a smirk on his face? Apart from that, he was his normal uncommunicative self and, as usual, continued to study his plate.

Days eight and nine. Our last two days at sea. All systems go on the long voyage back to Miami. Like everyone else, our final days at sea would be spent repeating the things we had most enjoyed doing during the week: swimming pools, sun decks, nursery, restaurants, sports or simply doing nothing. At the same time, the whole atmosphere was more subdued than usual and some people, no doubt mindful of the recent triple heist, huddled into small groups, looking furtively around and chatting in lowered voices.

At dinner on day eight, the Fords said they would happily take Tommy and put him to bed if we wanted to go to the theatre where they were showing an apparently brilliant performance of a West End spectacular. We dressed, said good night to Tommy and left the Fords playing with him in our stateroom. As we closed the door, he was giggling excitedly, watching Amanda doing a ventriloquist act with his teddy, chasing Jeremy round the table.

Day nine. The final evening. We packed our cases and left them outside the stateroom as requested, to be transported to the customs hall ready for us to disembark. In the light of the week's onshore events, we had been warned to expect considerable delays as all cases would be scanned and perhaps searched.

Tommy made sure we were up in time to watch the docking at 8 o'clock on our final morning. Three hours later we lined up at the appointed time and slowly made our way towards the gangway. As we stepped back on to terra firma we became conscious of the large number of armed security personnel and police officers scattered throughout the terminal building. We located our luggage fairly quickly and advanced towards a customs officer who waved down at Tommy as we approached. He reciprocated in kind, shrieked twice and brandished his teddy in the direction of the official. That did it; the man leaned down, shook hands with teddy, waved us through to the exit of the building and wished us a pleasant onward journey.

The next stage was to take us to Miami International Airport. We had arranged to share a minibus taxi with the Fords as they, too, were flying out later in the day. They cleared customs twenty minutes after us and together we went off to look for our transfer to the airport.

Having checked in our cases, we met up again at a point between our departure gates. We found a few empty seats at the side of the concourse and set our bags down on the marble floor between them. Our plane was due to leave a couple of hours before theirs and they insisted we go off and enjoy a coffee while they walked Tommy around as there was plenty for him to see. We said we would be back at 4 o'clock but turned up 10 minutes early.

When we got to within about 50 metres of our meeting place, we were alerted by the screams of a young child. Ours! We peered through the milling crowd in front of us and were horrified to see Jeremy Baker leaning over Tommy's buggy, forcibly taking the teddy from his grasp. He stepped back and, despite the child's protestations, violently snatched it away from him. What he did not realise was that I had attached it securely to the frame of the buggy that morning before leaving the ship so as not to risk losing it as we disembarked.

We saw the head of the teddy separate from the body and, in an instant, a shower of diamonds splashed down on to the marble surface and bounced off in every direction. Two armed guards who were standing nearby stepped up to see what was happening and quickly took control of the situation. My enduring memory of that day is watching the Fords, our erstwhile dining companions, being led away in handcuffs, heads bowed, by four burly police officers in the direction of a waiting vehicle.

The subsequent police investigation revealed that, for three years, Jeremy Ford had worked as a hypnotist, touring provincial theatres. He had used his knowledge of the art to convince the salespersons in the various jewellers' to go into a back room and fill a small black velvet bag with a selection of diamonds.

That had been the easy part.

MY LITTLE GUY

He was only 5 years old but for me he was the best company a man could ask for. Like every other grandad, I suppose, I felt that our relationship was special, unique.

My wife had passed away just three weeks before my daughter, Amelia, gave birth to Matty and, as my son-in-law had already lost both his parents, that left me in a very special position as the only grandparent. I was missing my wife dreadfully and perhaps in some ways I was just trying to fill a void but Matty instantly became of paramount importance to me. With his big, blue eyes and blond hair, he was a very happy little boy.

Fortunately I was still very active and I wanted to help Amelia in any way that I could. Apart from shopping and a few obvious chores like vacuuming and even a little cooking, I tried my hand at washing baby clothes and sterilising just about everything. After a while I felt particularly daring and changed my first nappy. It turned out to be the first of many but at least those newfangled disposable things are pretty easy to operate.

The only problem was that I lived some distance across town and no longer ran a car. Occasionally I slept in Amelia's spare bedroom but that arrangement was far from ideal. For some time my wife and I had been thinking about selling up the house and downsizing as we no longer needed so much space. On my own, I certainly didn't, and when a two-bedroom apartment became available in Amelia's block I couldn't resist finding out more. It really seemed ideal for me as it was on the ground floor with a small garden; just right for when old age really kicks in. After very little hesitation we decided I should put in an offer. I did. It was accepted and within one month I took up residence in my new abode. I was determined not to make a nuisance of myself and to keep my distance but at least I was on hand whenever needed.

It gave me so much pleasure to watch little Matty develop: his first smile, laughing, sitting up, crawling, toddling and, before I knew it, starting to walk. I enjoyed rocking him to sleep, putting him down in his bed, taking him on my lap, pushing him in his buggy and generally just spending time with him, playing with puzzles, Lego, cars and spacemen. Over time we developed a very close bond, both physical and affective.

By the time he was three, he could manage the stairs and, as they lived on the floor above, he started to pay me regular visits, at first with his mother but then on his own; mind you, she did phone me every time to say he was on his way down! Every day he would come down, usually in the afternoon, to read all the classics with me: Pinocchio, Snow White, The Three Bears, Winnie the Pooh, to name but a few.

Round about his fourth birthday we graduated to more serious themes and, in addition to all the normal subjects like animals, transport, spacemen and football, we started to have some real man-to-man conversations. 'My Little Guy,' as I had started to call him, used to sit on my lap or cuddle in beside me on the sofa and not just listen to me but make his own comments too. I know all Grandads would say the same thing but Matty was a very bright little chap and was starting to handle abstract ideas and, like all youngsters, to ask a lot of questions.

One day we were kicking a football around in my garden and I had just explained to him that he would not be seeing my brother, 'Uncle Mac,' again as he had just died. That, of course, was a difficult one for him.

"Where is he then, Grandad?"

"Well, I think he's up in Heaven," I replied.

He was pensive for a moment, then looked up and asked, "Oh. And where's that?"

That was a difficult one for me this time. "Well, it's way up there, somewhere beyond the sky, Little Guy."

He seemed a bit puzzled by that but five minutes later, when he noticed a distant plane towing a long vapour trail across the deep blue sky, he tugged at my sleeve, pointed into the air and asked, "Grandad. Is that Uncle Mac coming back?"

I think my heart missed a beat or two but I soon picked up when he looked at me again and asked,

"Grandad. If I'm your Little Guy, does that mean you're my Big Guy?"

"Well, yes. I guess we're just two guys together really," I replied.

It seemed that overnight he was coming up for the grand old age of five. Where had the time gone? We now discussed more serious and abstract notions like friendship, loyalty and suffering - naturally not in so many words, but in simple terms related to his own experience and he appeared to absorb much of what he heard. He was interested in everything I mentioned and there wasn't much we didn't talk about (but we did avoid politics and religion as we wanted to remain friends!)

When we talked about icebergs and flooding, deserts and drought and the fact that drinking water might one day run out, there was a genuine look of concern on his face. He appeared to be really worried at the thought of no drinking water and I was sorry I had broached the subject.

The following day, however, I understood the reason for his concern when, as usual, he came down to see me. I heard him coming along the corridor and waited while he padded up to the door. As I opened it, I indulged him in one of our standard jokes. "The door's opening. That must be the postman." And then, as our eyes met, "Oh no, it's Matty! Hello, Little Guy."

"Hello, Big Guy," came the reply.

He closed the door and stretched out his hands.

"This is for you, Grandad," he said proudly.

He was holding a present he had brought me. It was shaped very much like a bottle and, indeed, it was an old soft drinks bottle but he had wrapped it carefully in tinfoil to make it a surprise for me. I thanked him and started to peel back the tinfoil. He twitched with excitement, looked up at me with his big blue eyes and said, half under his breath, "I hope you like it, Grandad. Keep it in a safe place."

With bated breath, I removed the tinfoil and discovered a bottle of clear water. He was bursting to explain to me what it was for. "I screwed the top on very tight," he began, "so that the water can't come out. It's in case that drought thing you told me about yesterday happens sooner than you think. Then you'll be OK because you'll have a whole bottle of water to keep you safe."

That was two days ago. Now I am struggling with a mixture of emotions. I feel very proud and fulfilled, yet at the same time sad and already a little bit lonely. Next week my Little Guy is going to start school.

Not to worry, though; Amelia told me this morning that number two is well on the way and should be here within the next five months.

www.ingramcontent.com/pod-product-compliance
Lightning Source LLC
Chambersburg PA
CBHW060612130626
46555CB00002B/507